Coloring Books for Adults Relaxation

Beautiful Ladies Warriors, Gift for Men, Teens, Anti-stress Coloring Book

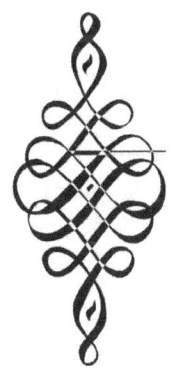

I Love Coloring

2017

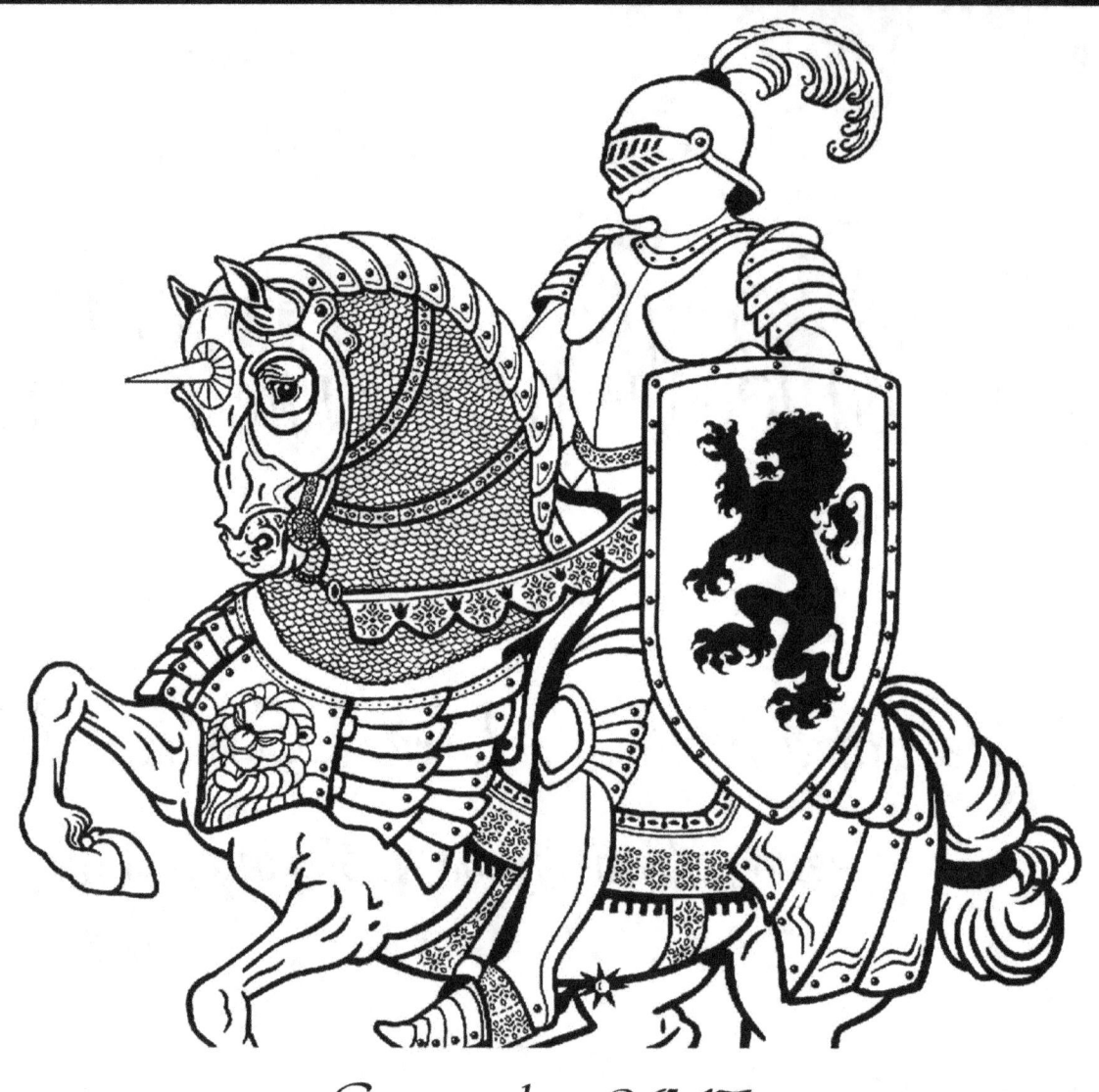

Copyright 2017

Coloring Gifts Volume 2

ISBN-13: 978-1545432013   ISBN-10: 1545432015

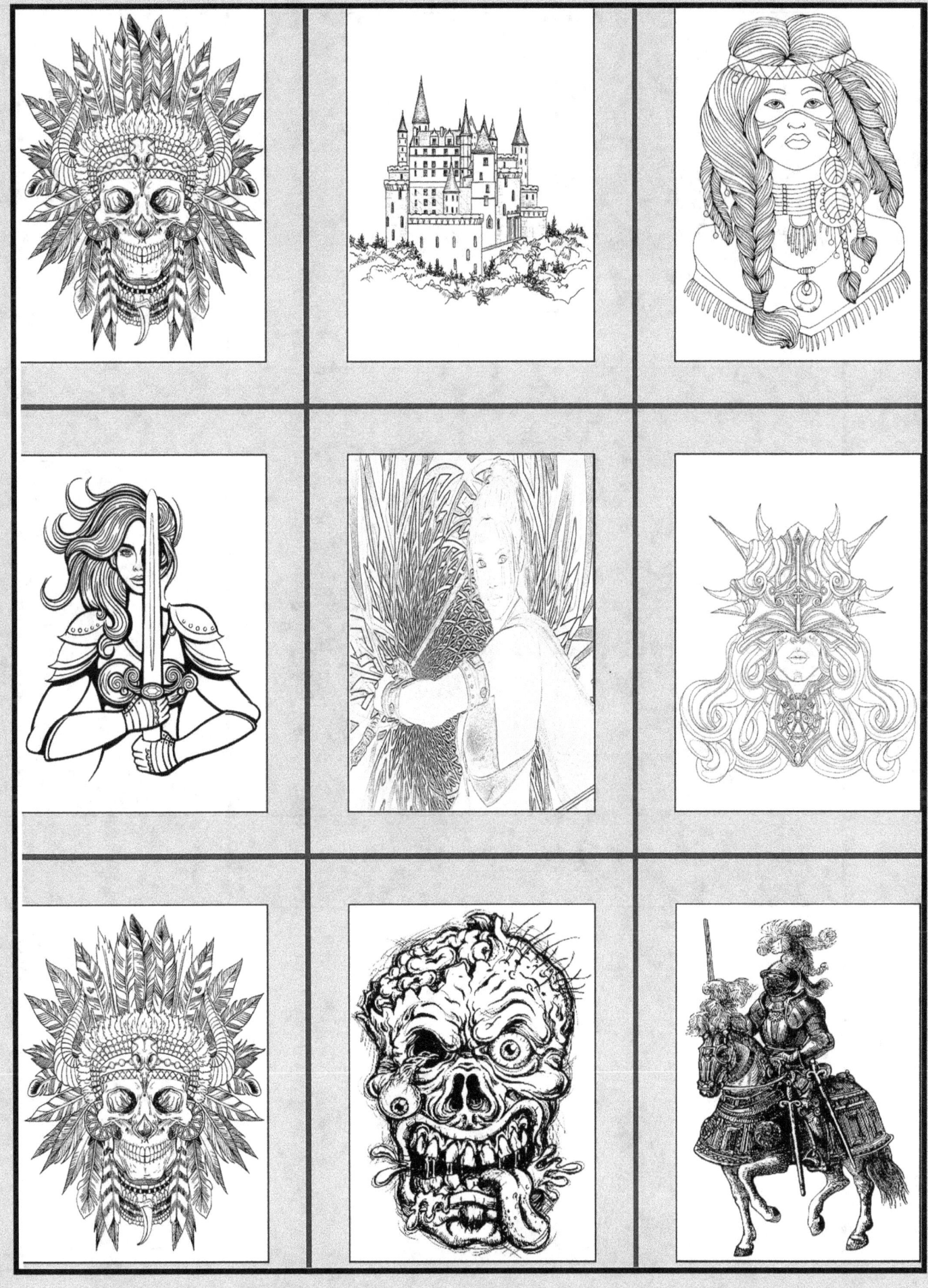

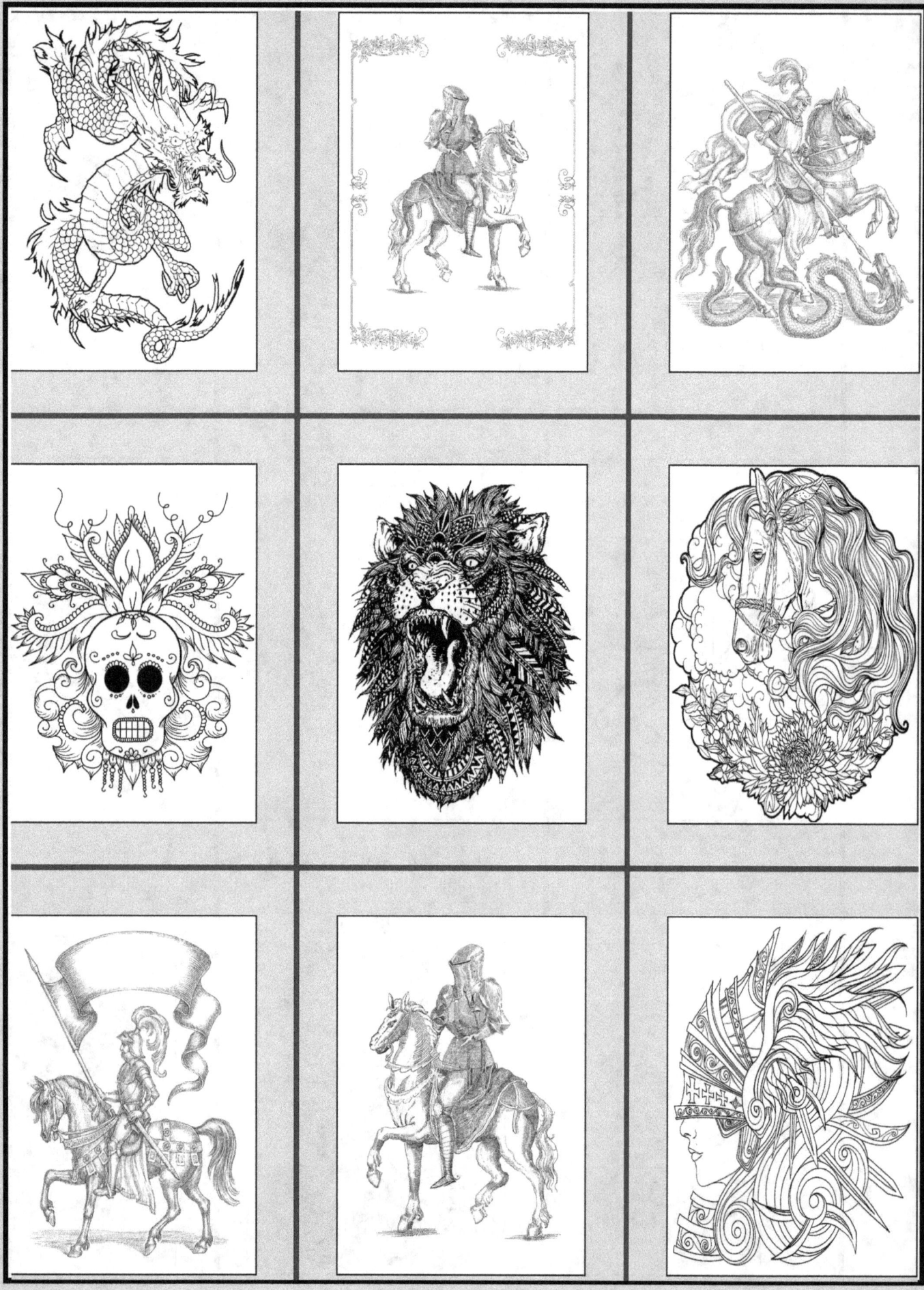

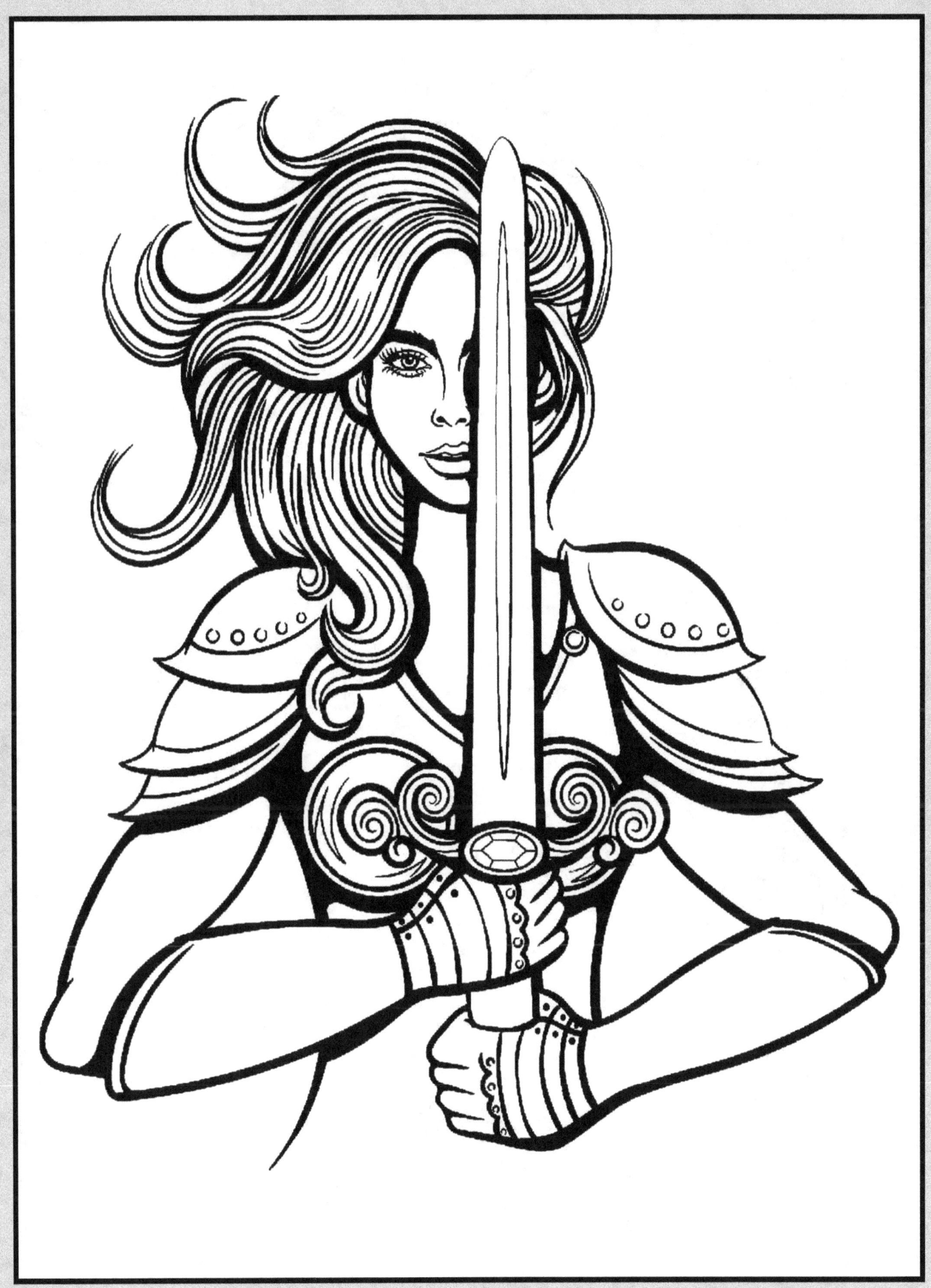

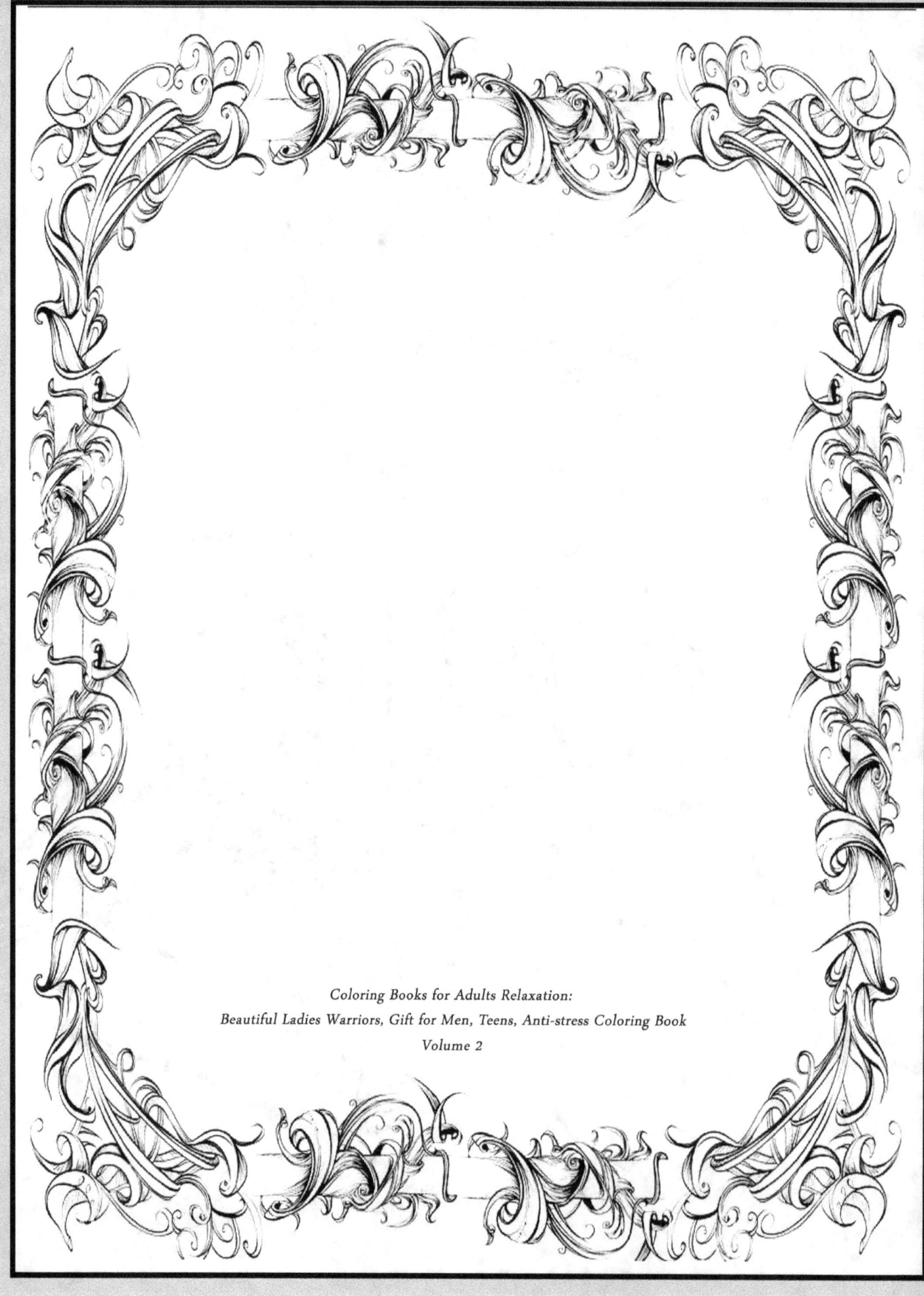

Coloring Books for Adults Relaxation:
Beautiful Ladies Warriors, Gift for Men, Teens, Anti-stress Coloring Book
Volume 2

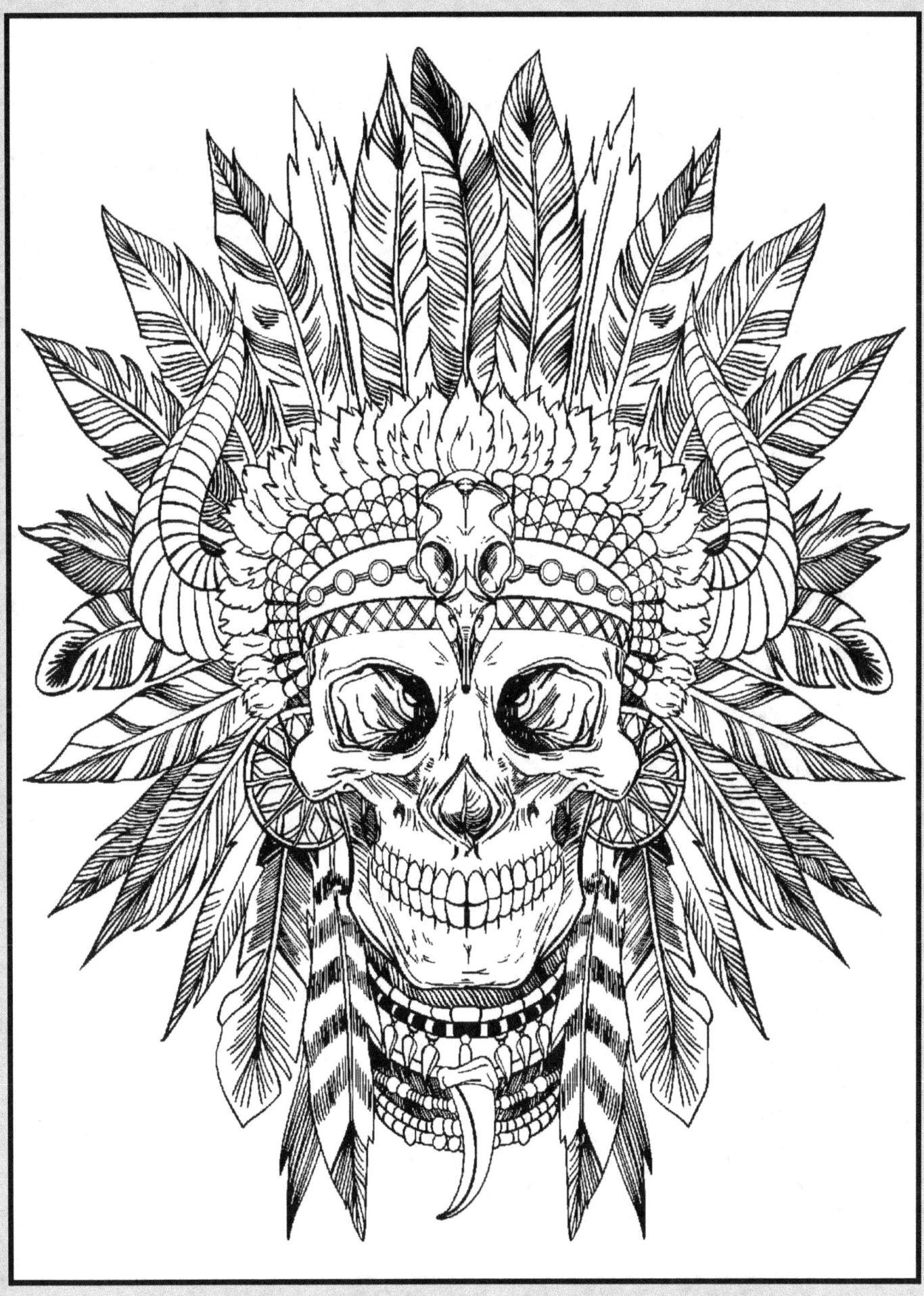

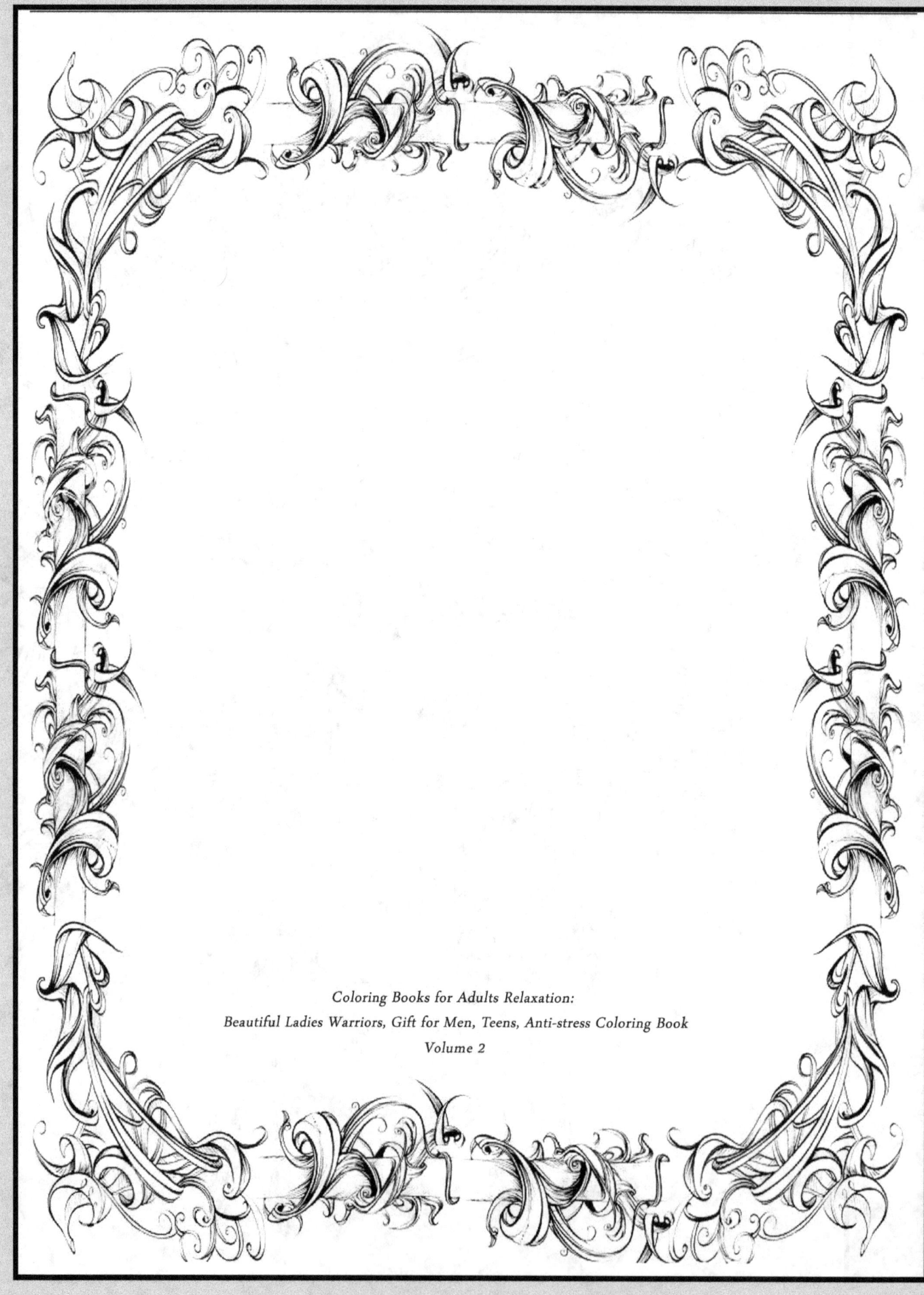

Coloring Books for Adults Relaxation:
Beautiful Ladies Warriors, Gift for Men, Teens, Anti-stress Coloring Book
Volume 2

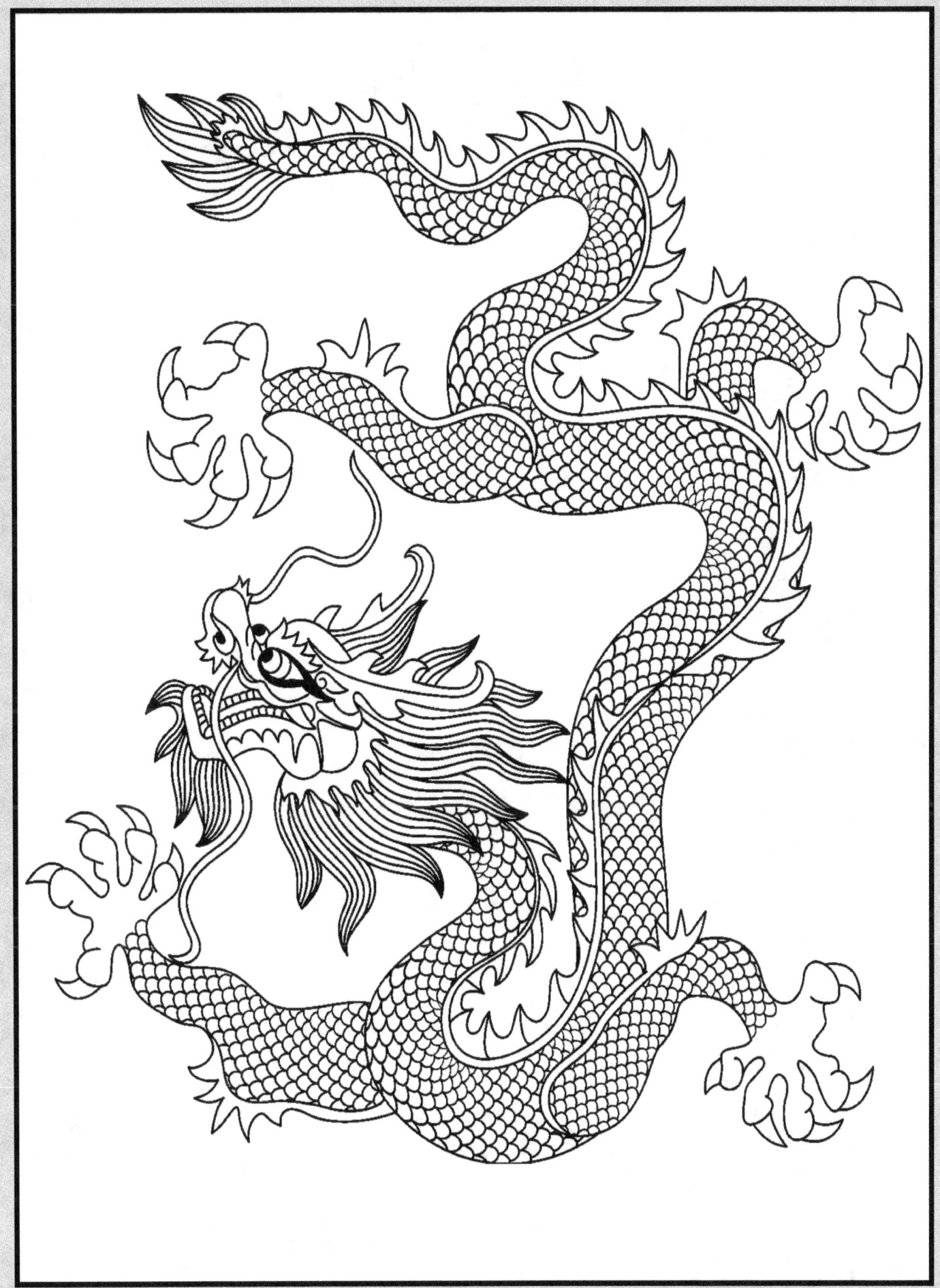

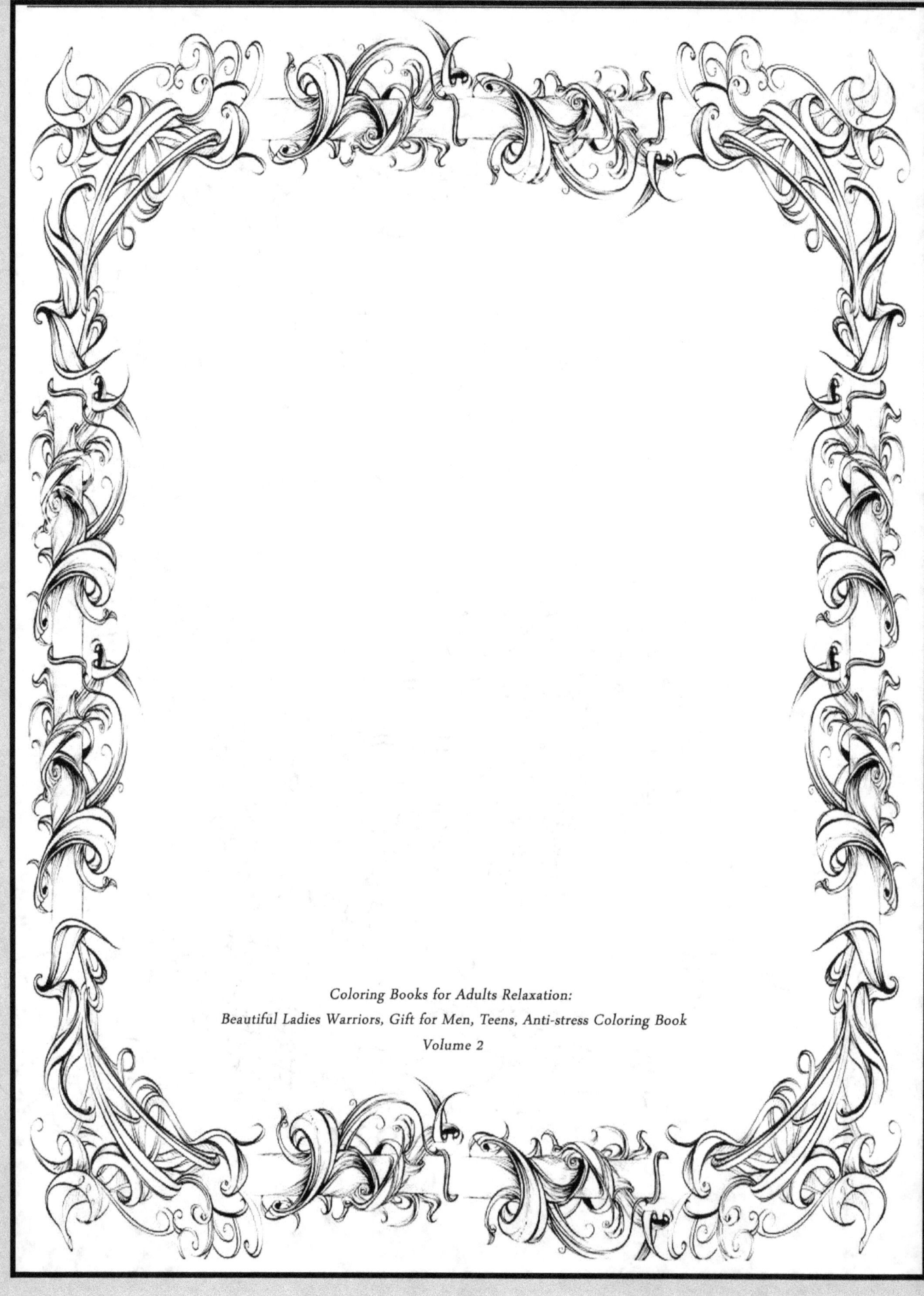

Coloring Books for Adults Relaxation:
Beautiful Ladies Warriors, Gift for Men, Teens, Anti-stress Coloring Book
Volume 2

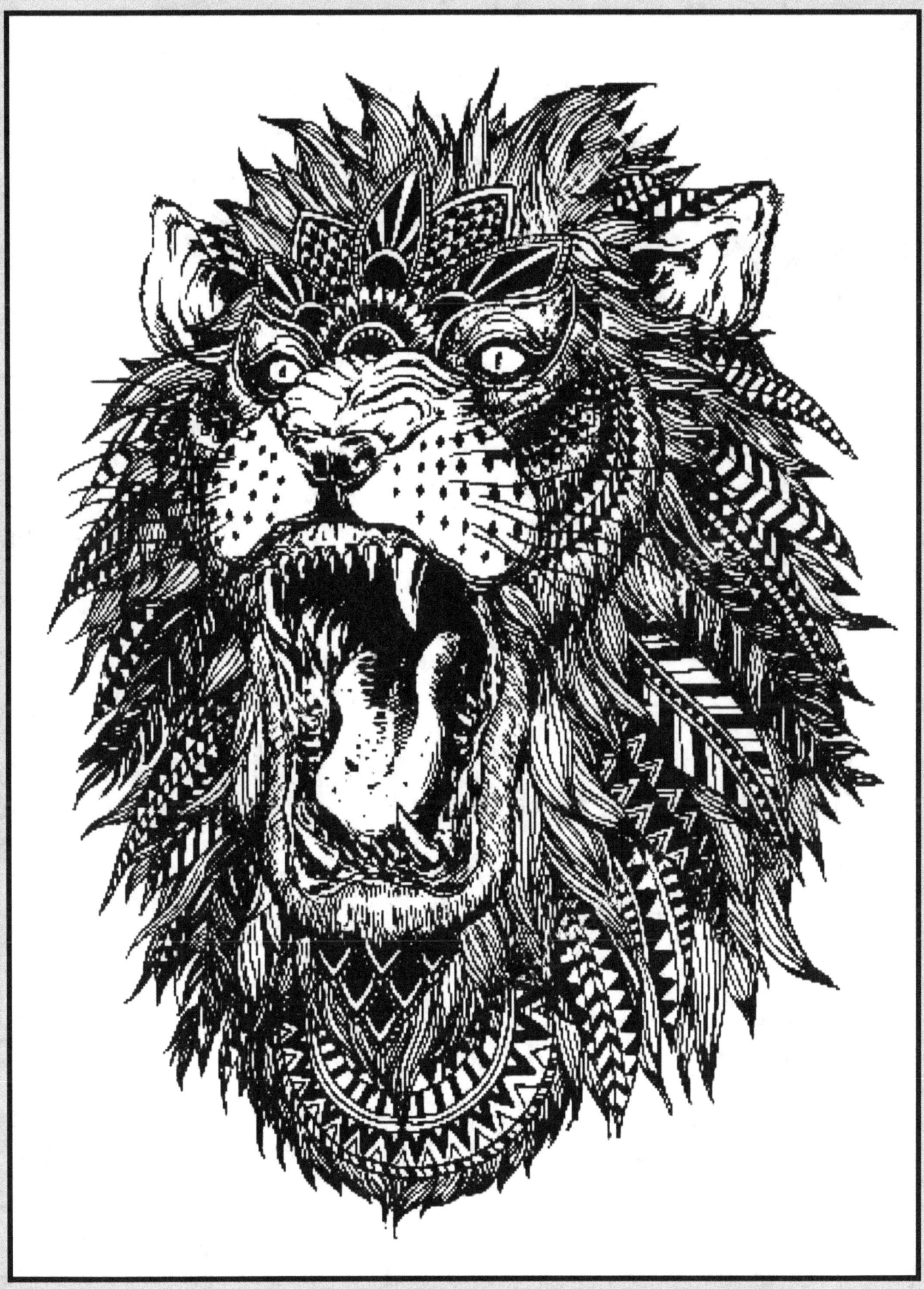

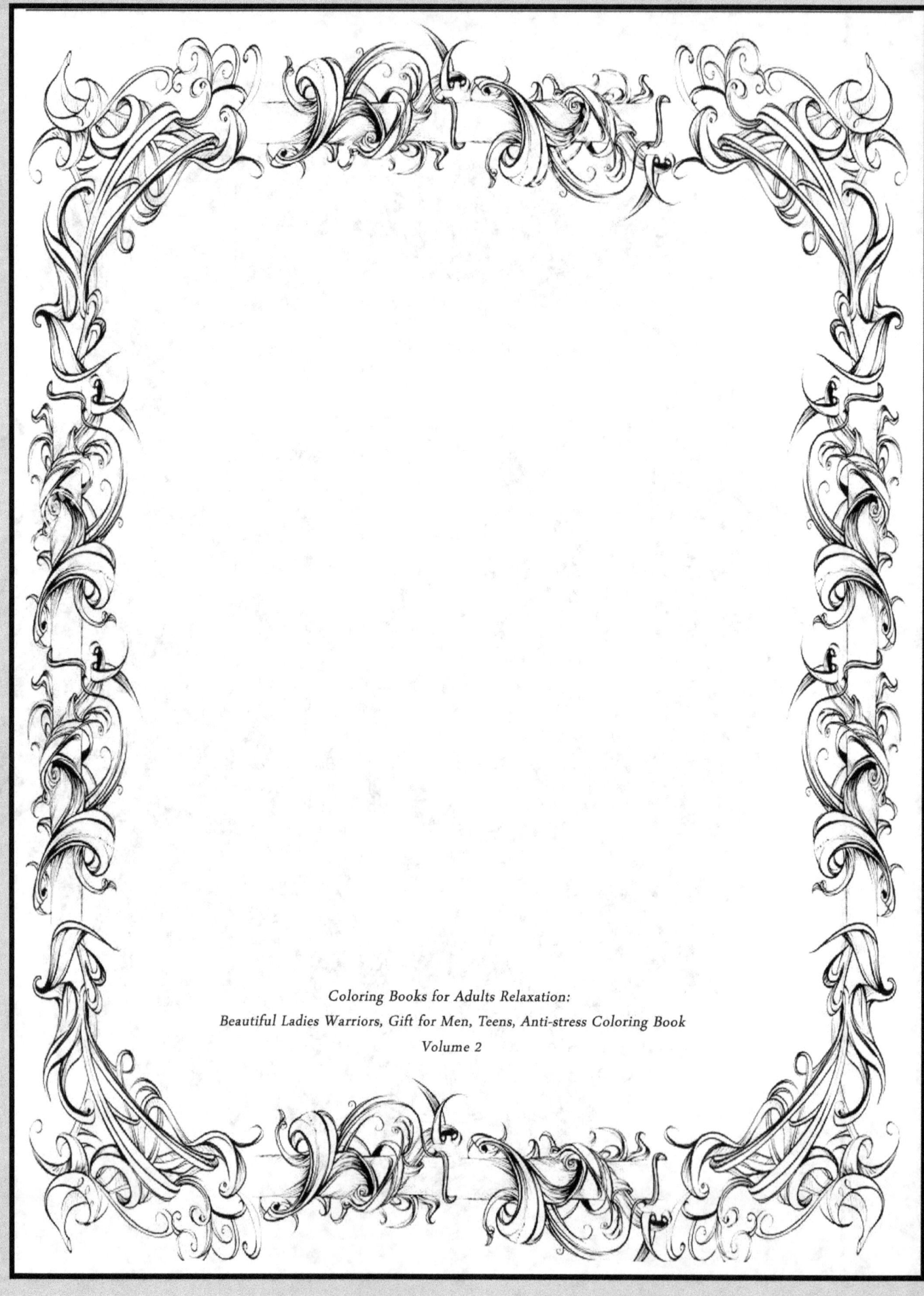

Coloring Books for Adults Relaxation:
Beautiful Ladies Warriors, Gift for Men, Teens, Anti-stress Coloring Book

Volume 2

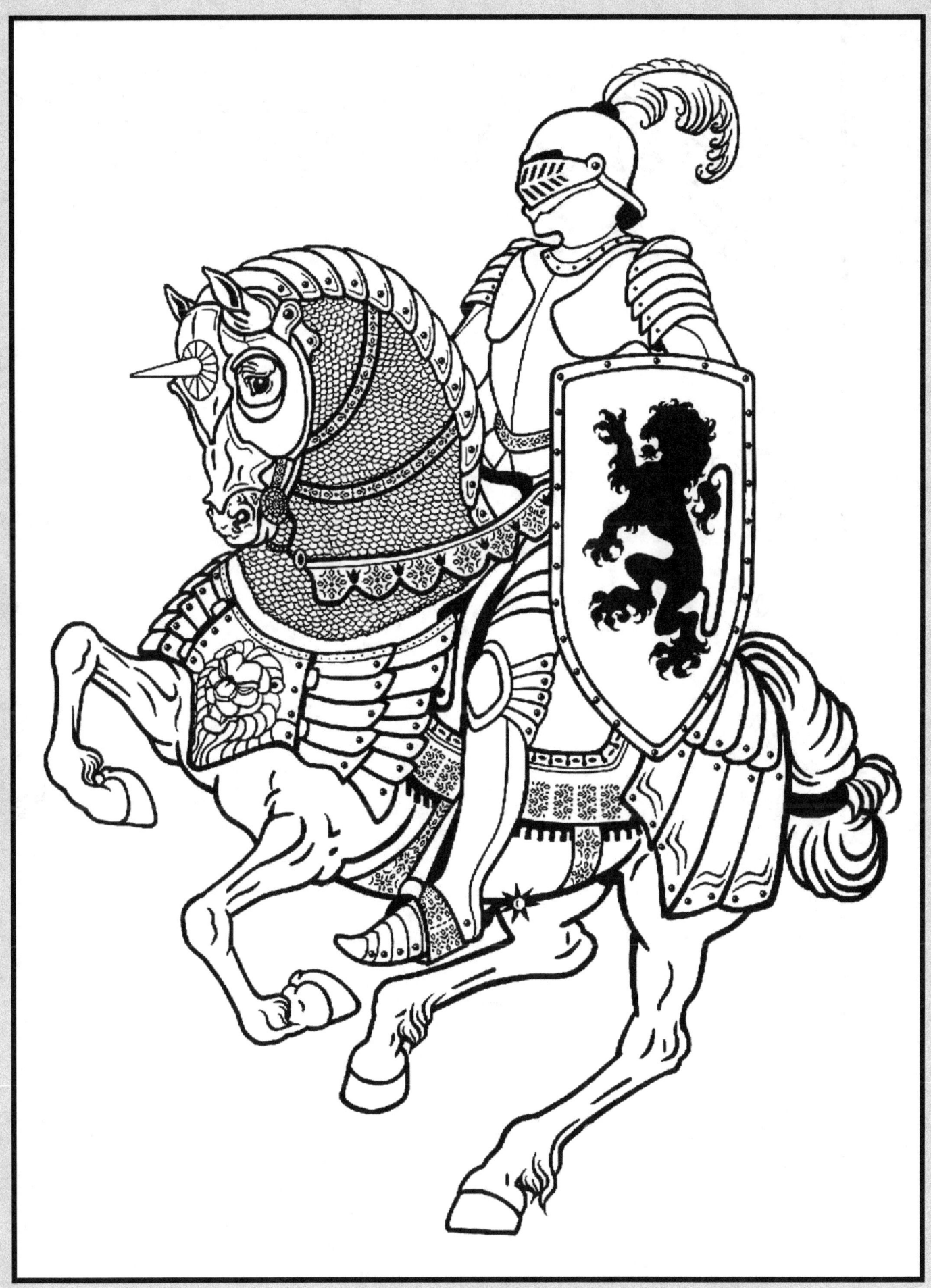

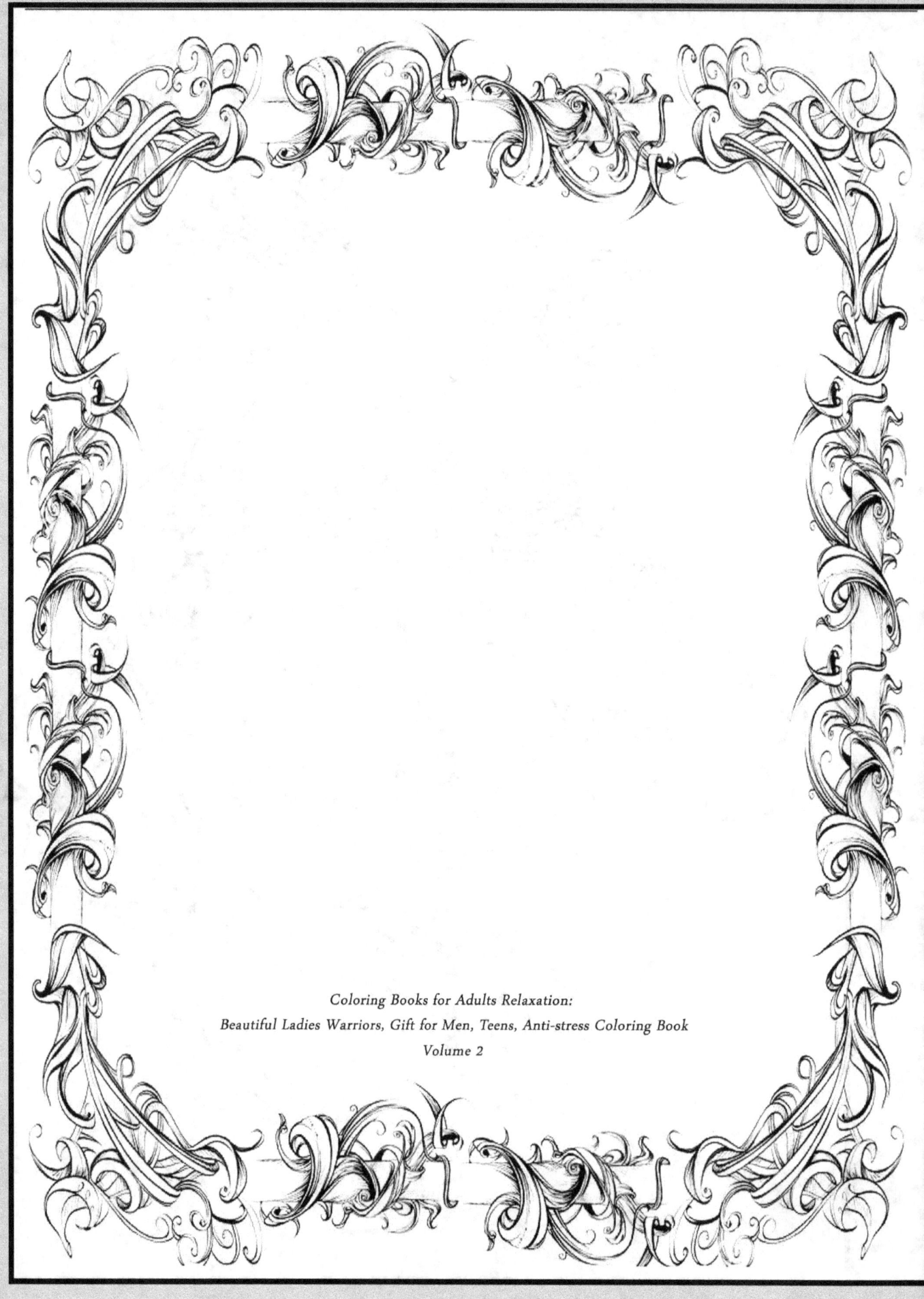

Coloring Books for Adults Relaxation:
Beautiful Ladies Warriors, Gift for Men, Teens, Anti-stress Coloring Book
Volume 2

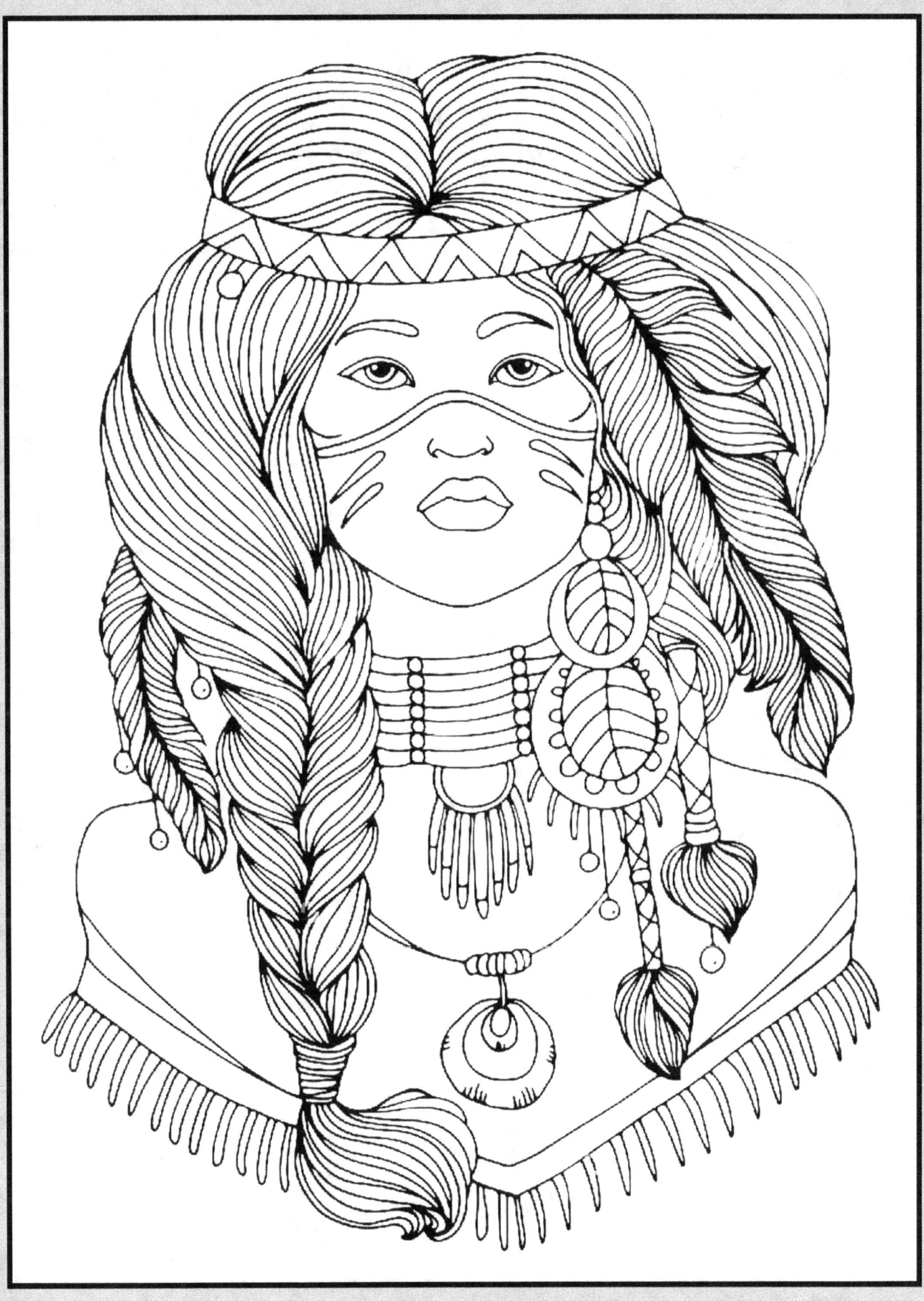

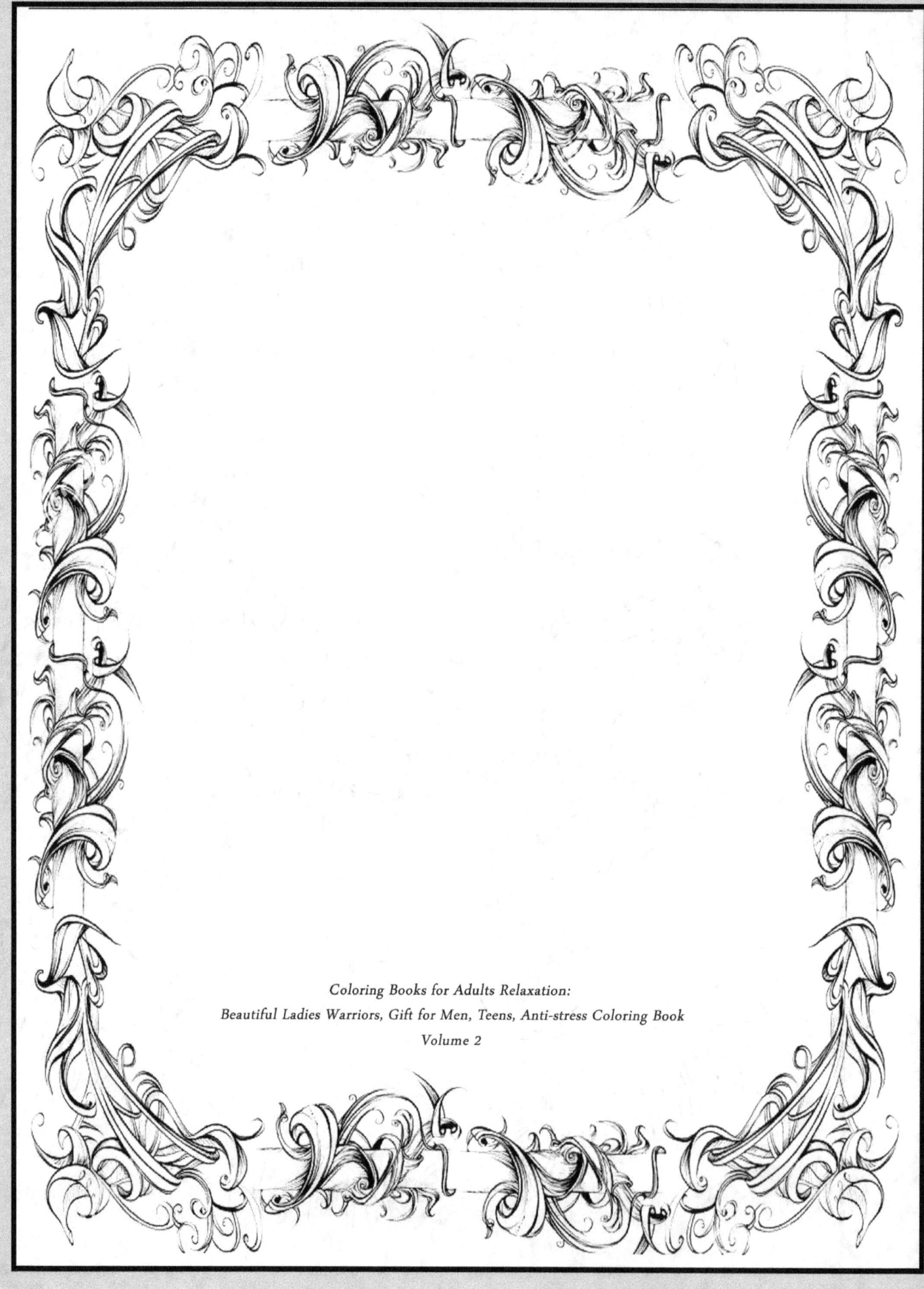

Coloring Books for Adults Relaxation:
Beautiful Ladies Warriors, Gift for Men, Teens, Anti-stress Coloring Book

Volume 2

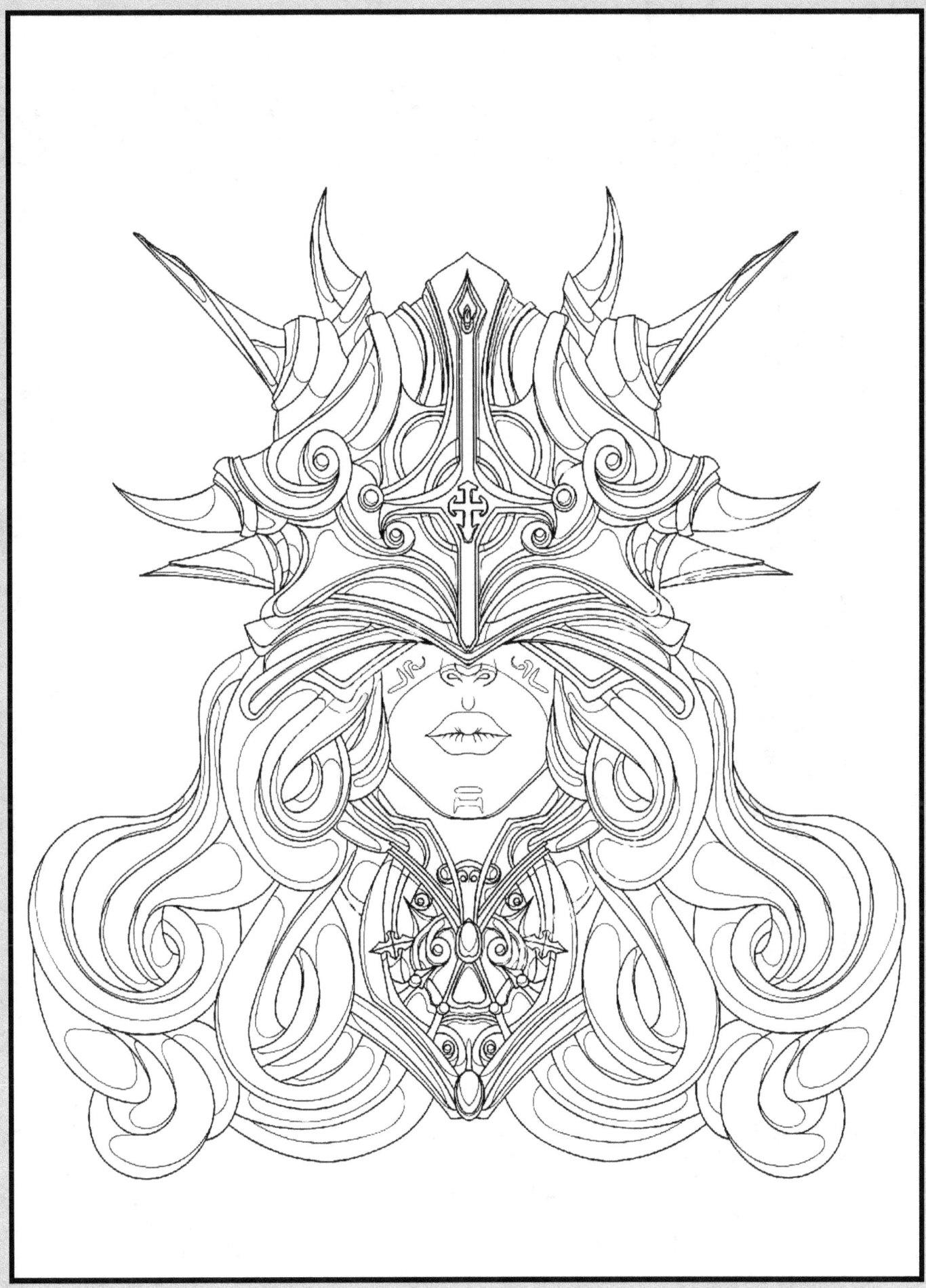

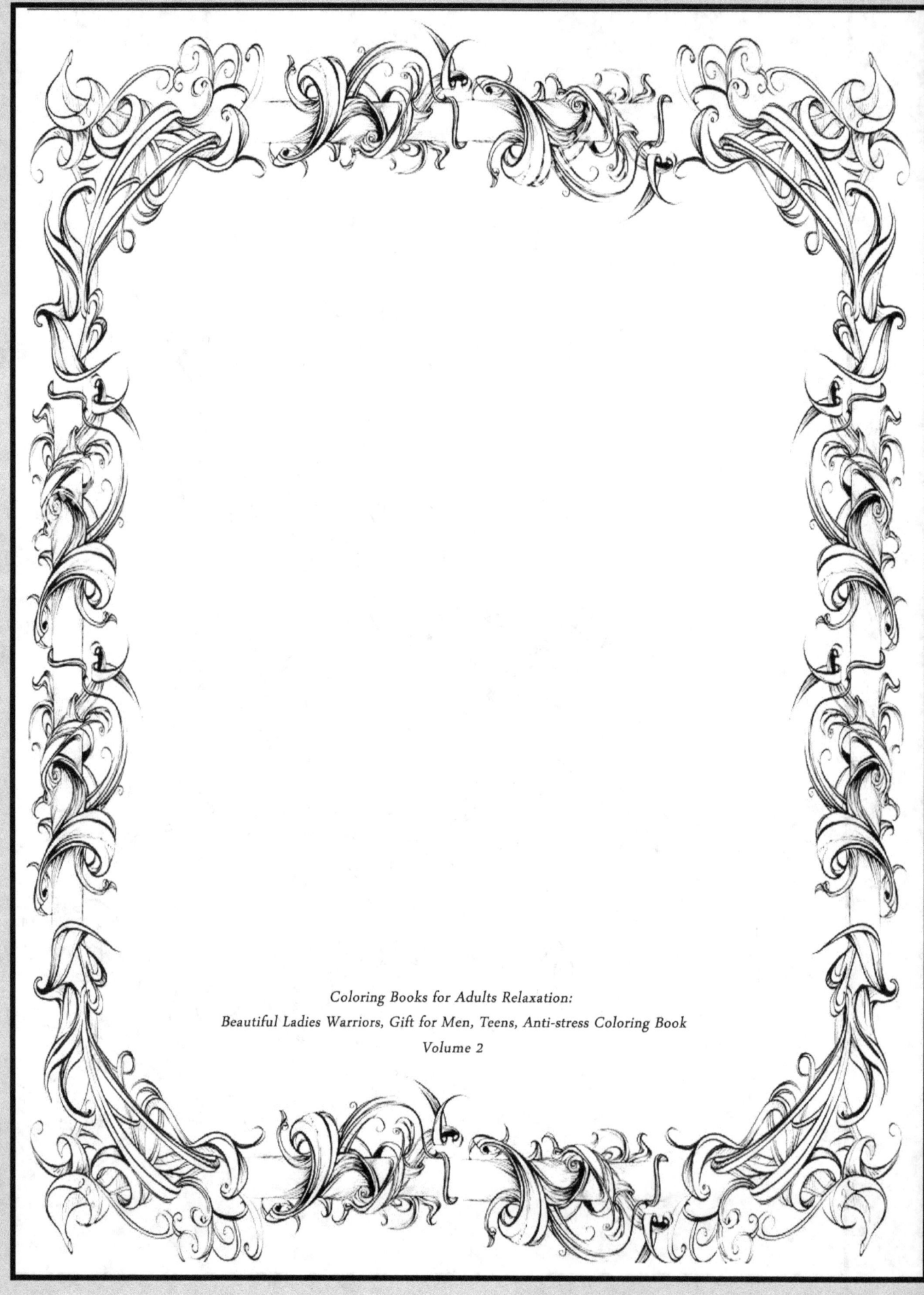

Coloring Books for Adults Relaxation:
Beautiful Ladies Warriors, Gift for Men, Teens, Anti-stress Coloring Book
Volume 2

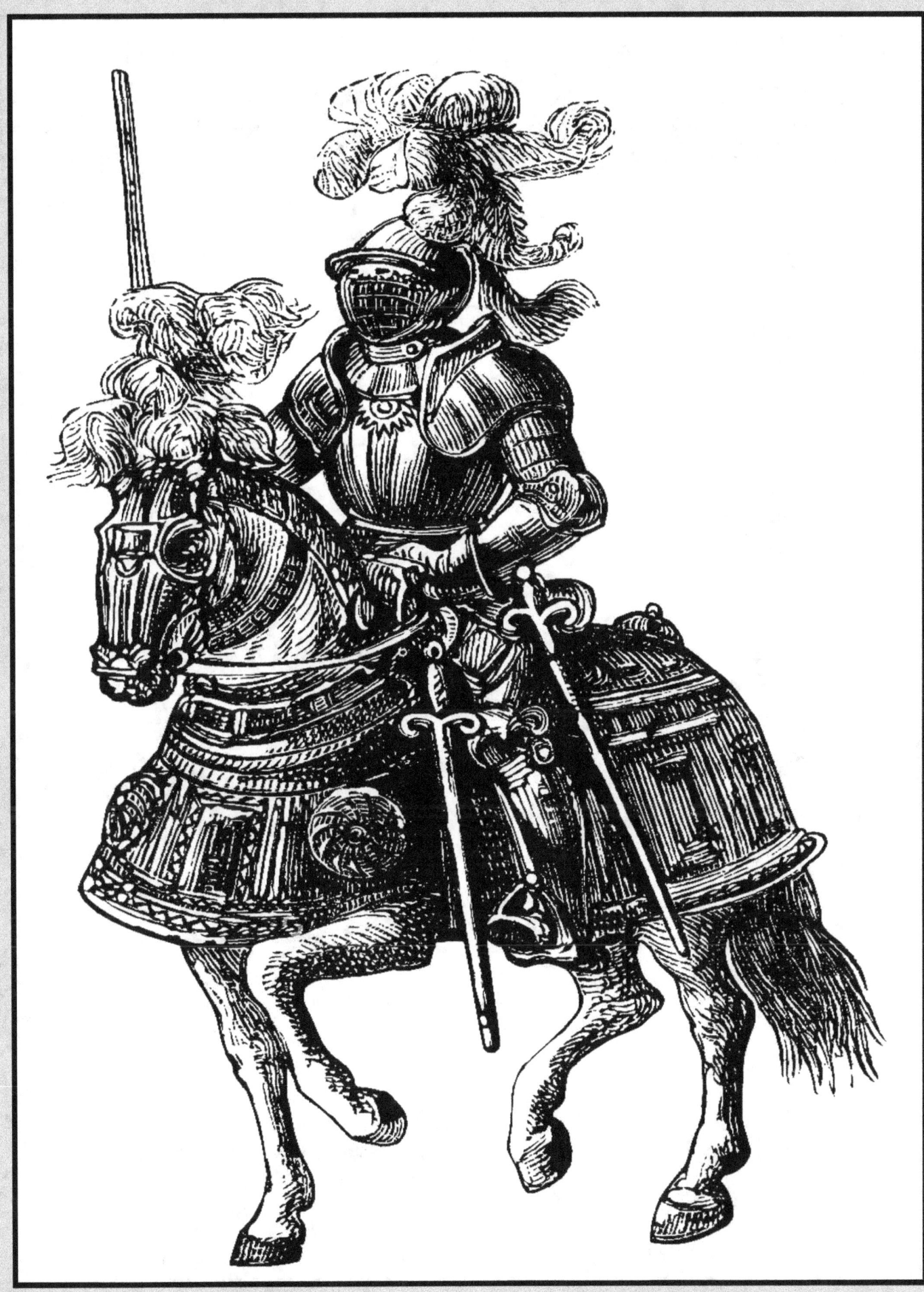

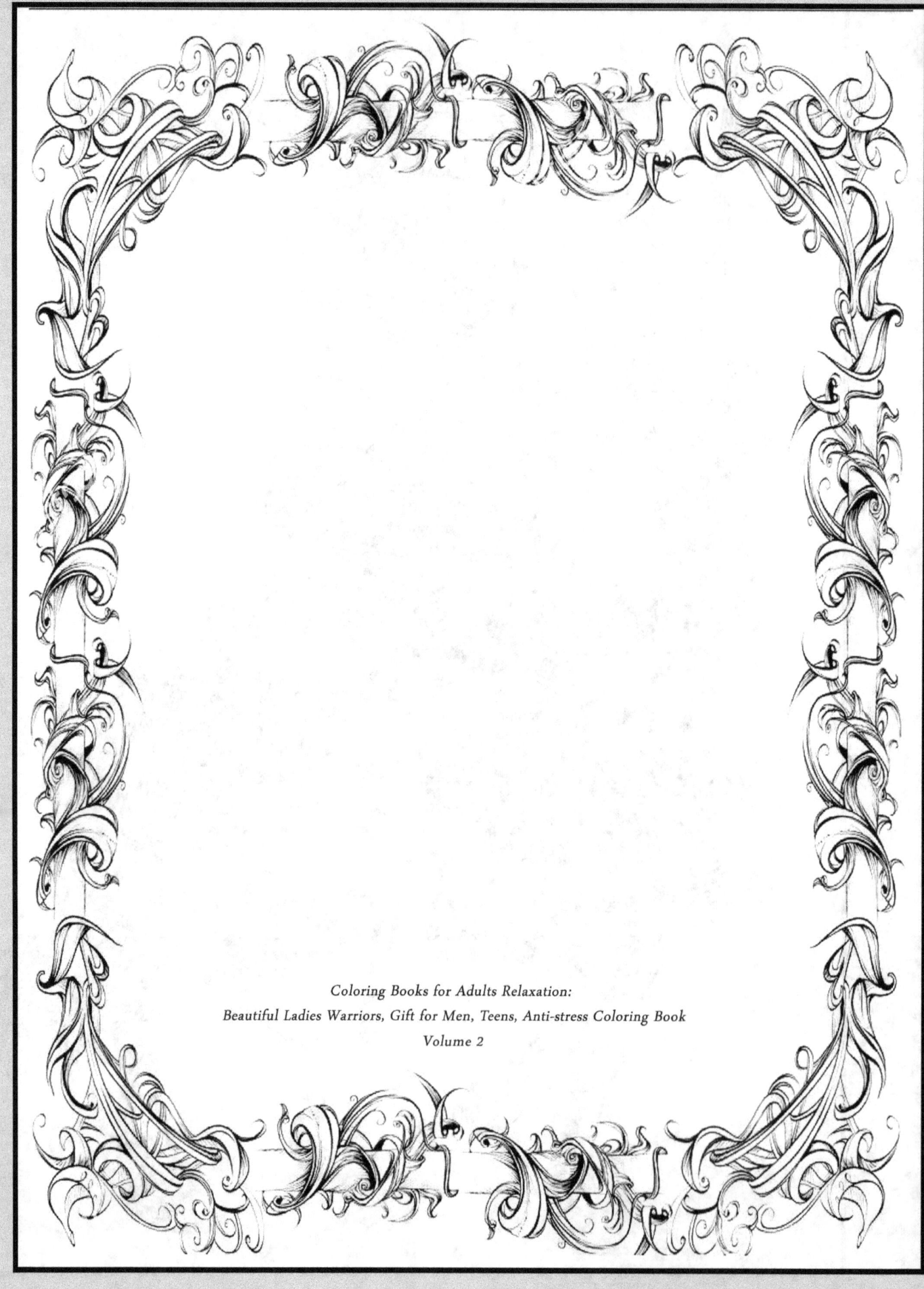

Coloring Books for Adults Relaxation:
Beautiful Ladies Warriors, Gift for Men, Teens, Anti-stress Coloring Book

Volume 2

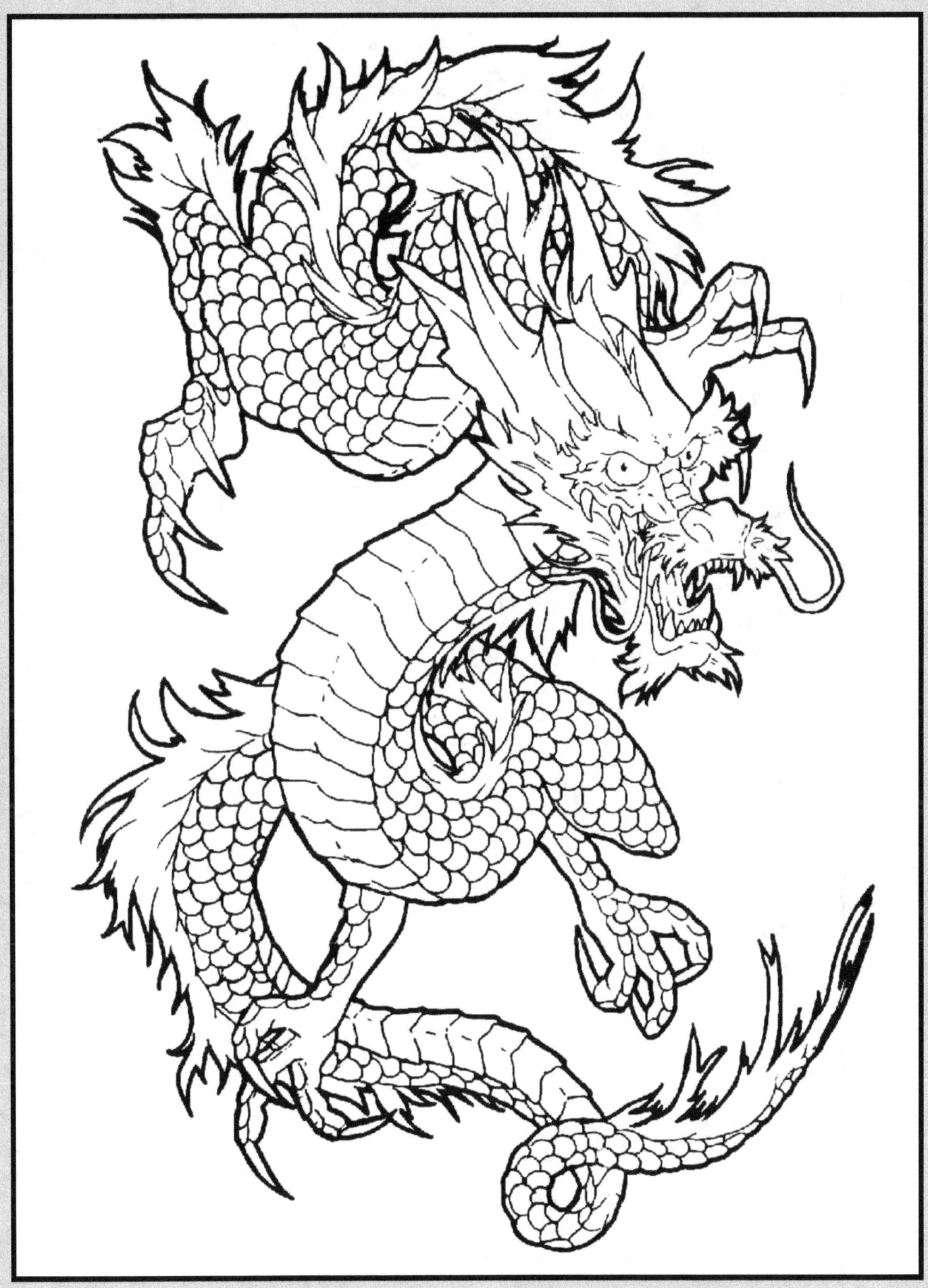

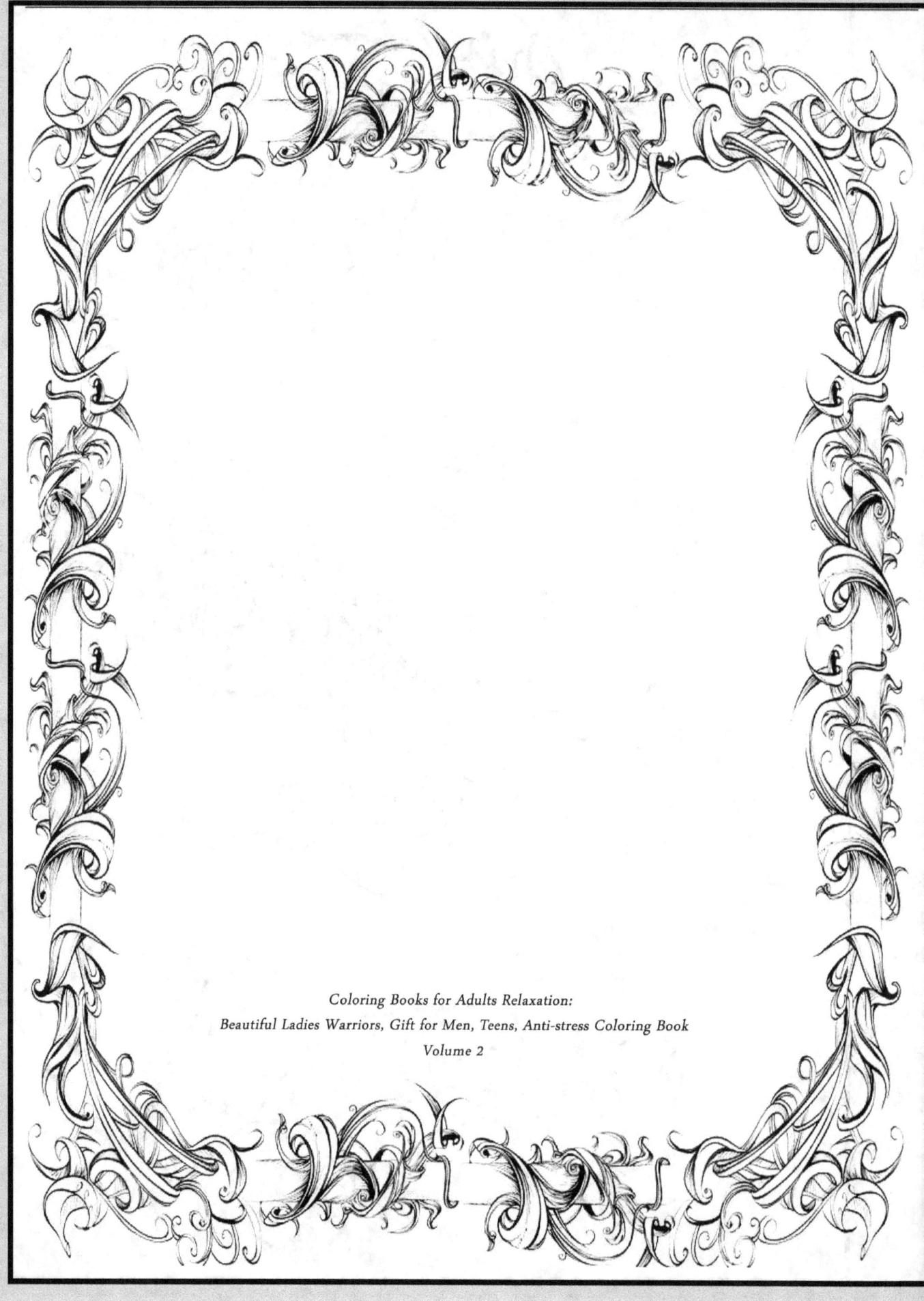

Coloring Books for Adults Relaxation:
Beautiful Ladies Warriors, Gift for Men, Teens, Anti-stress Coloring Book
Volume 2

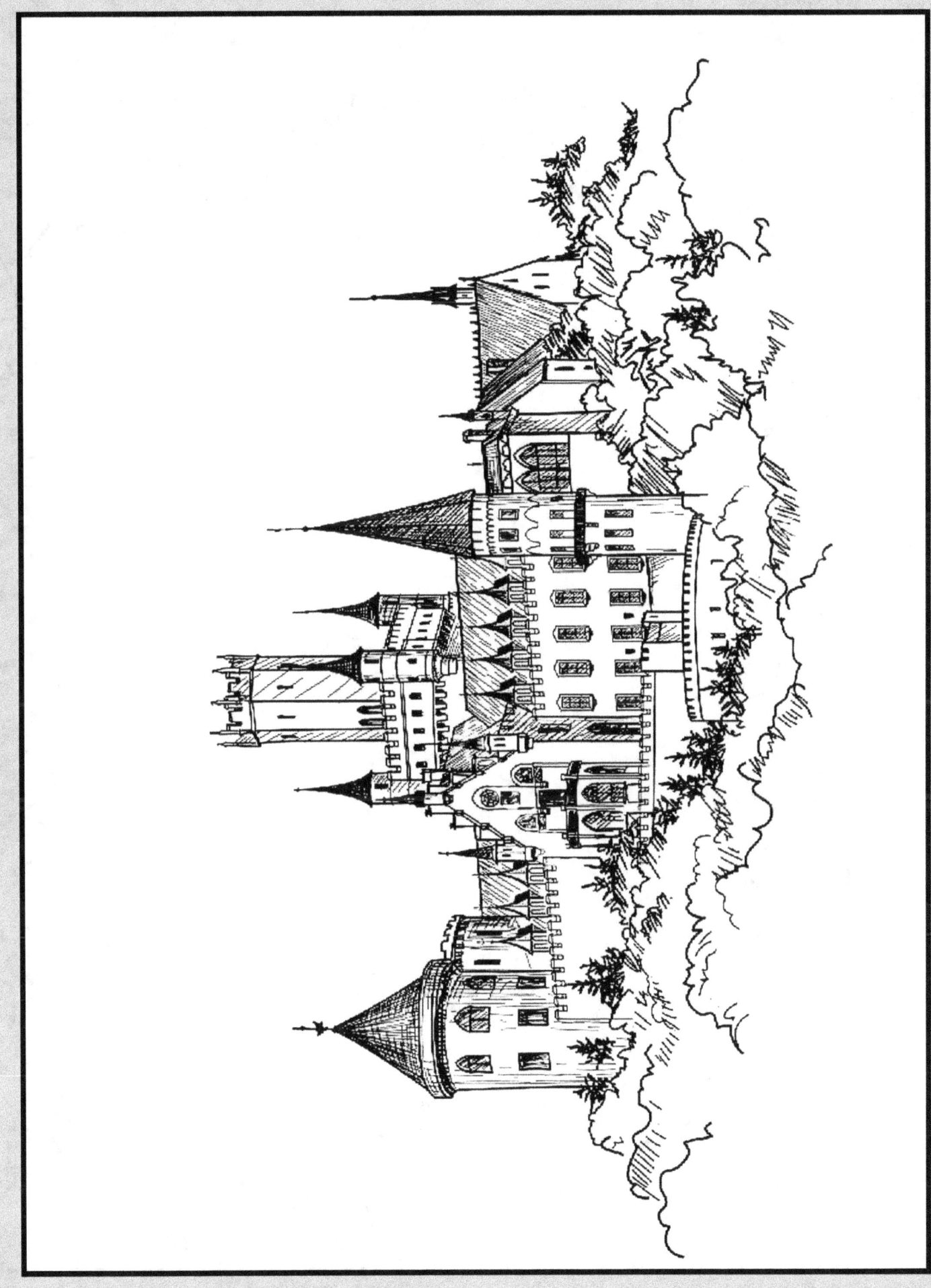

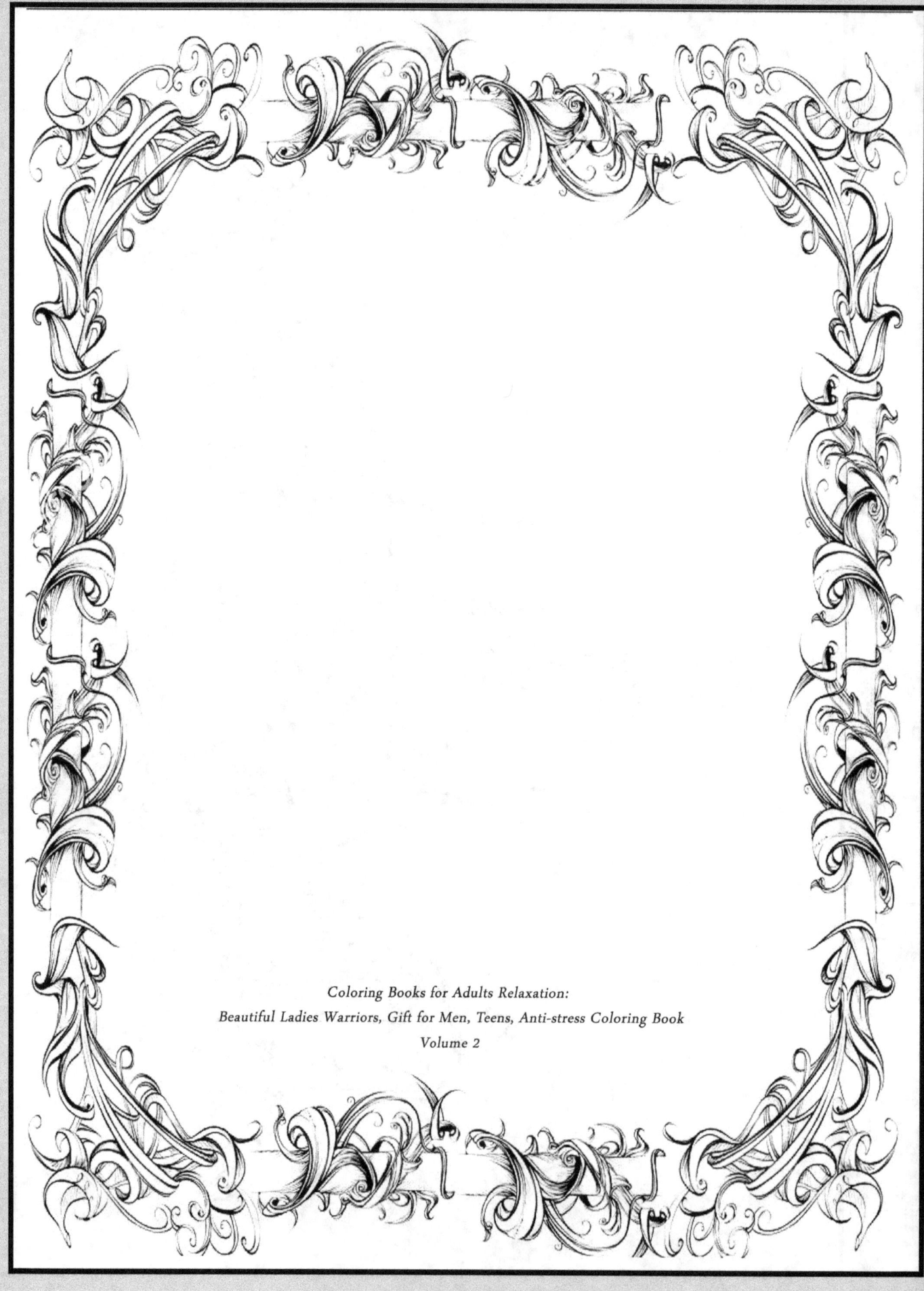

Coloring Books for Adults Relaxation:
Beautiful Ladies Warriors, Gift for Men, Teens, Anti-stress Coloring Book
Volume 2

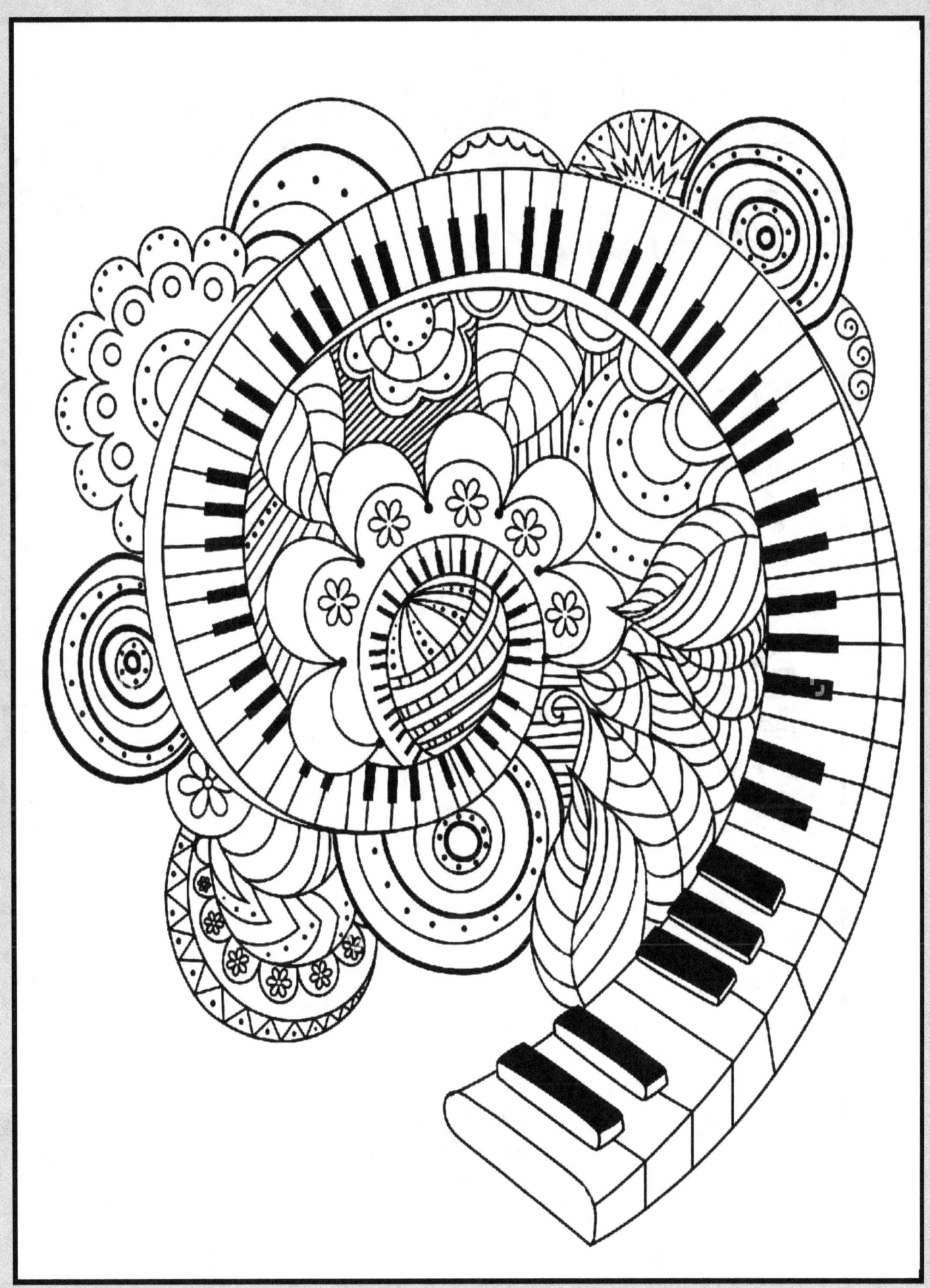

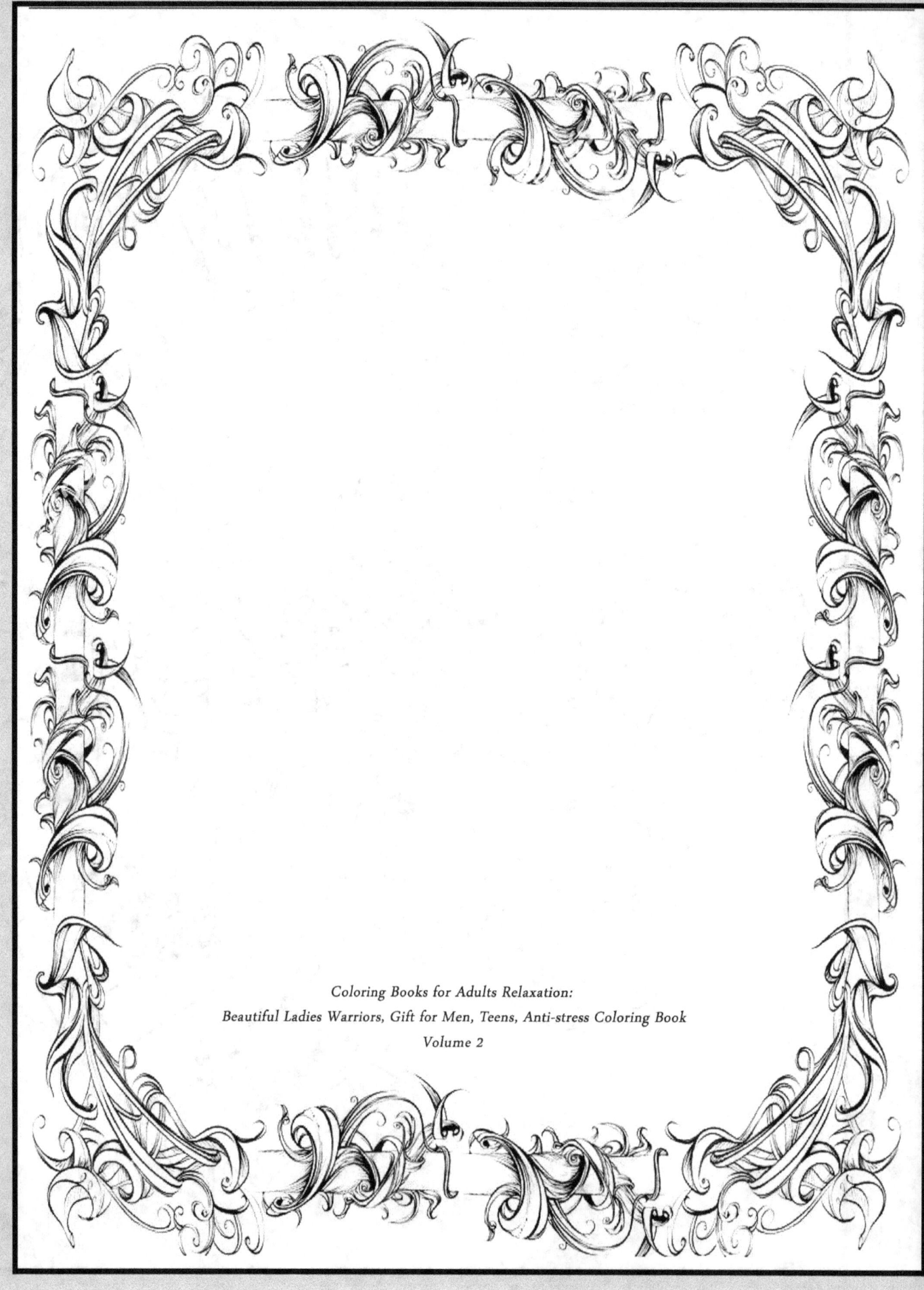

Coloring Books for Adults Relaxation:
Beautiful Ladies Warriors, Gift for Men, Teens, Anti-stress Coloring Book
Volume 2

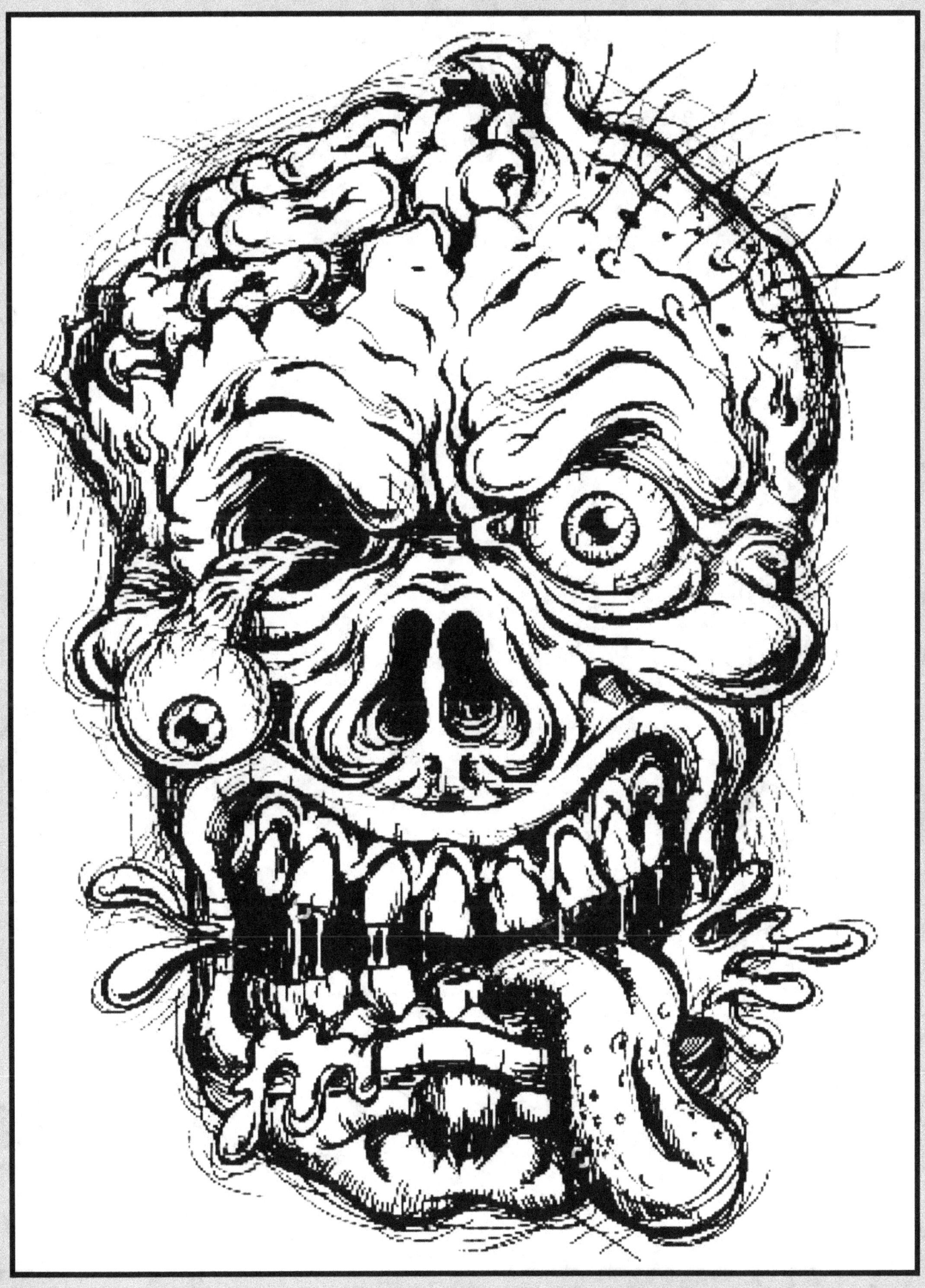

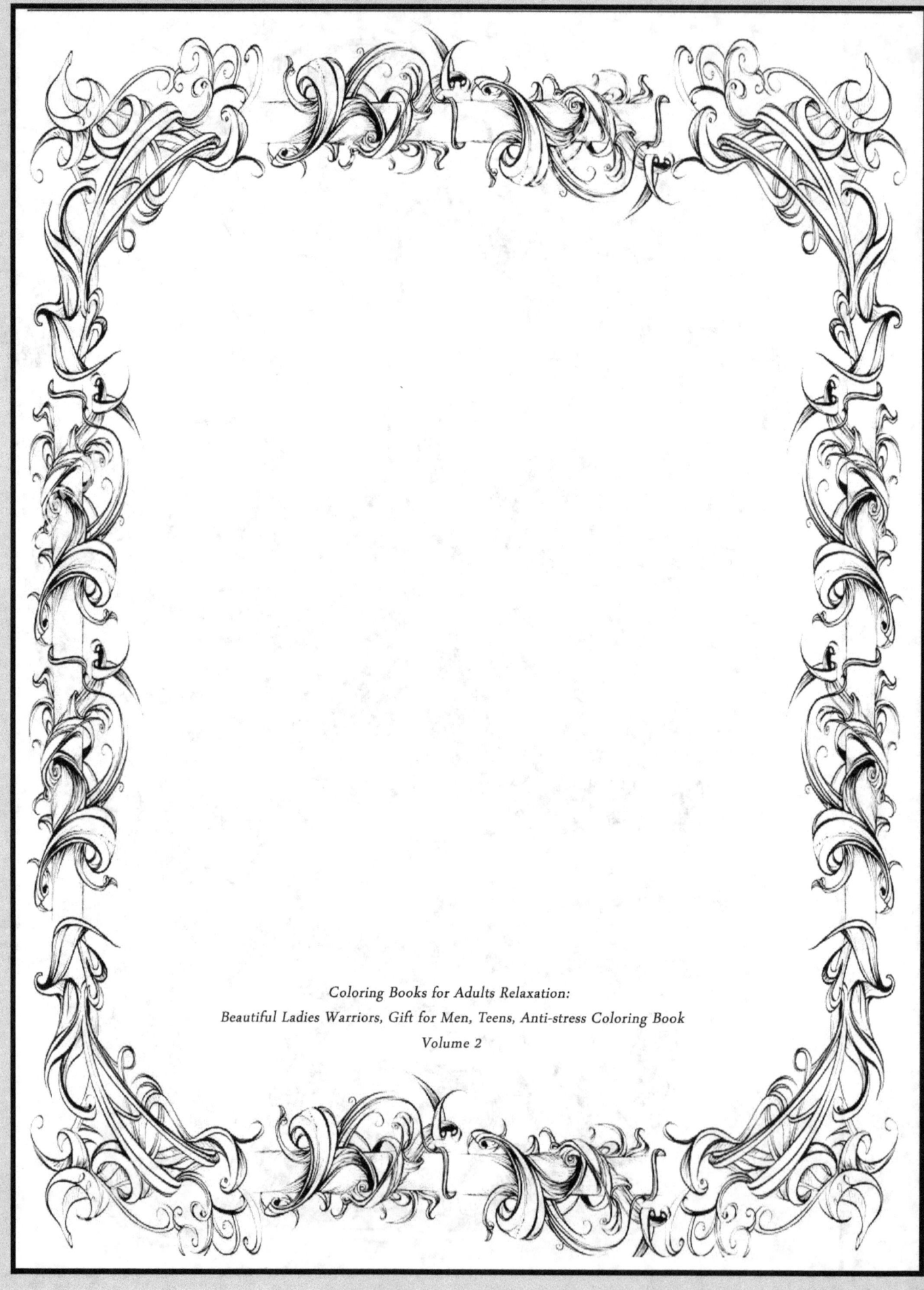

Coloring Books for Adults Relaxation:
Beautiful Ladies Warriors, Gift for Men, Teens, Anti-stress Coloring Book

Volume 2

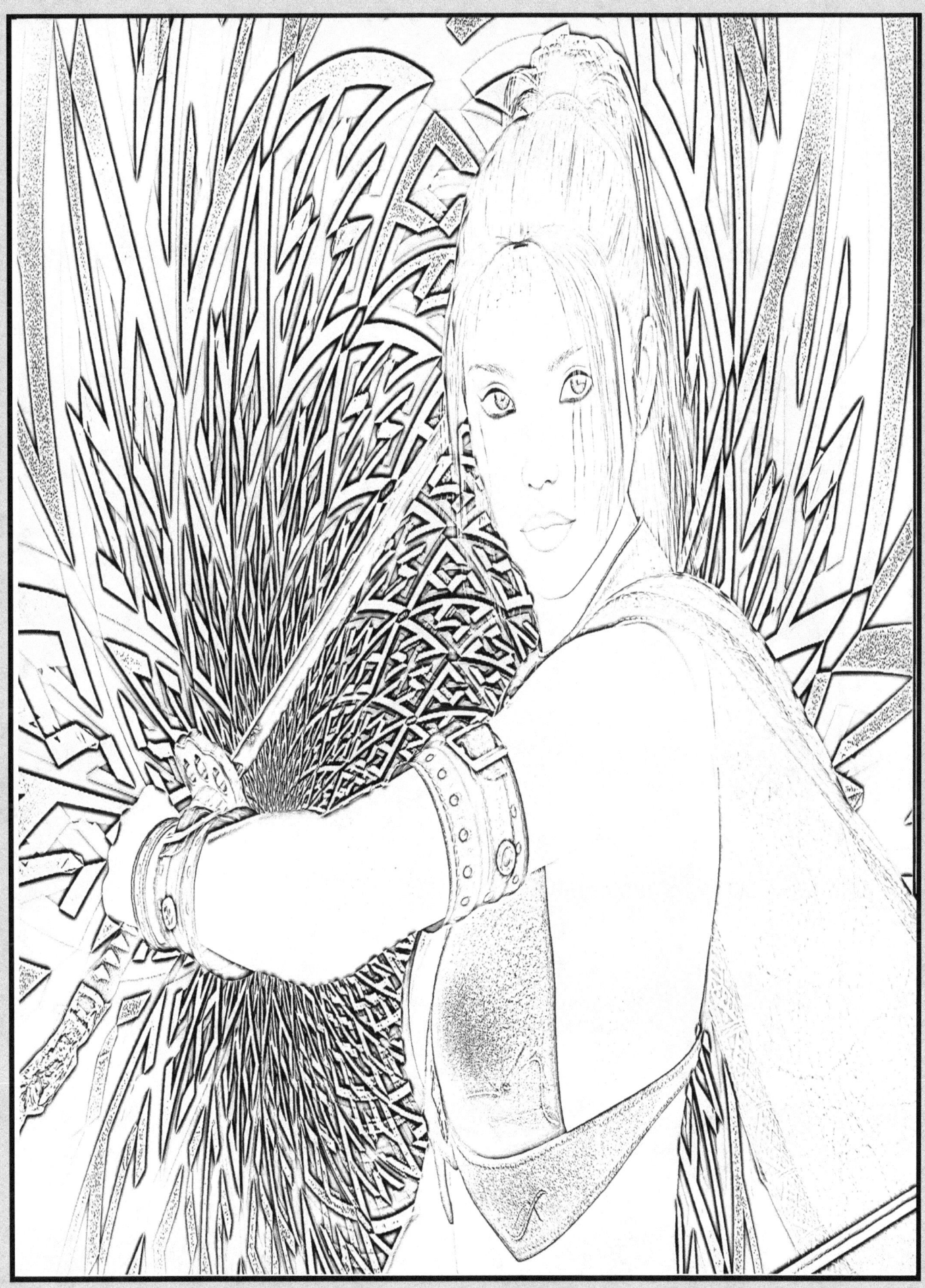

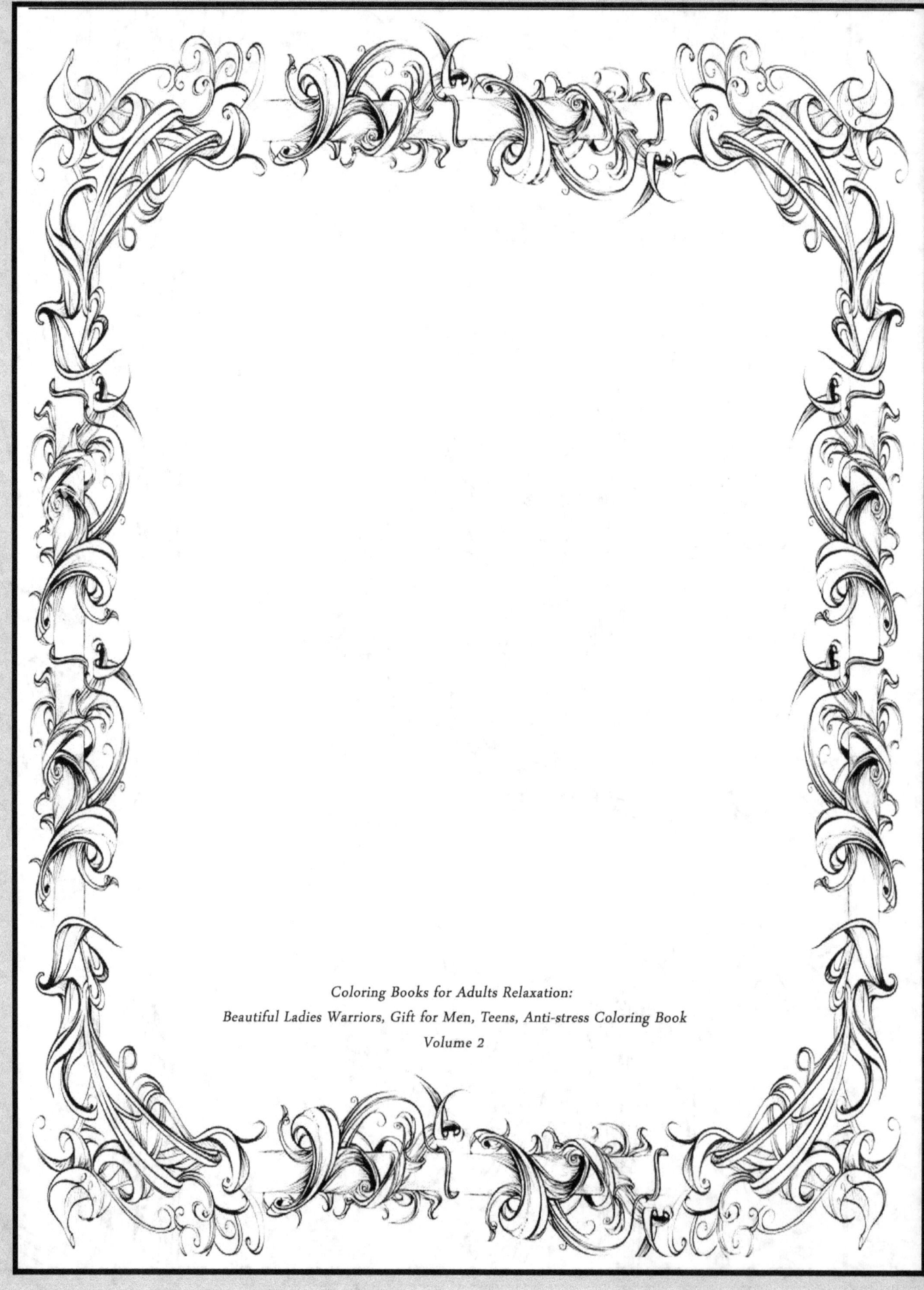

Coloring Books for Adults Relaxation:
Beautiful Ladies Warriors, Gift for Men, Teens, Anti-stress Coloring Book
Volume 2

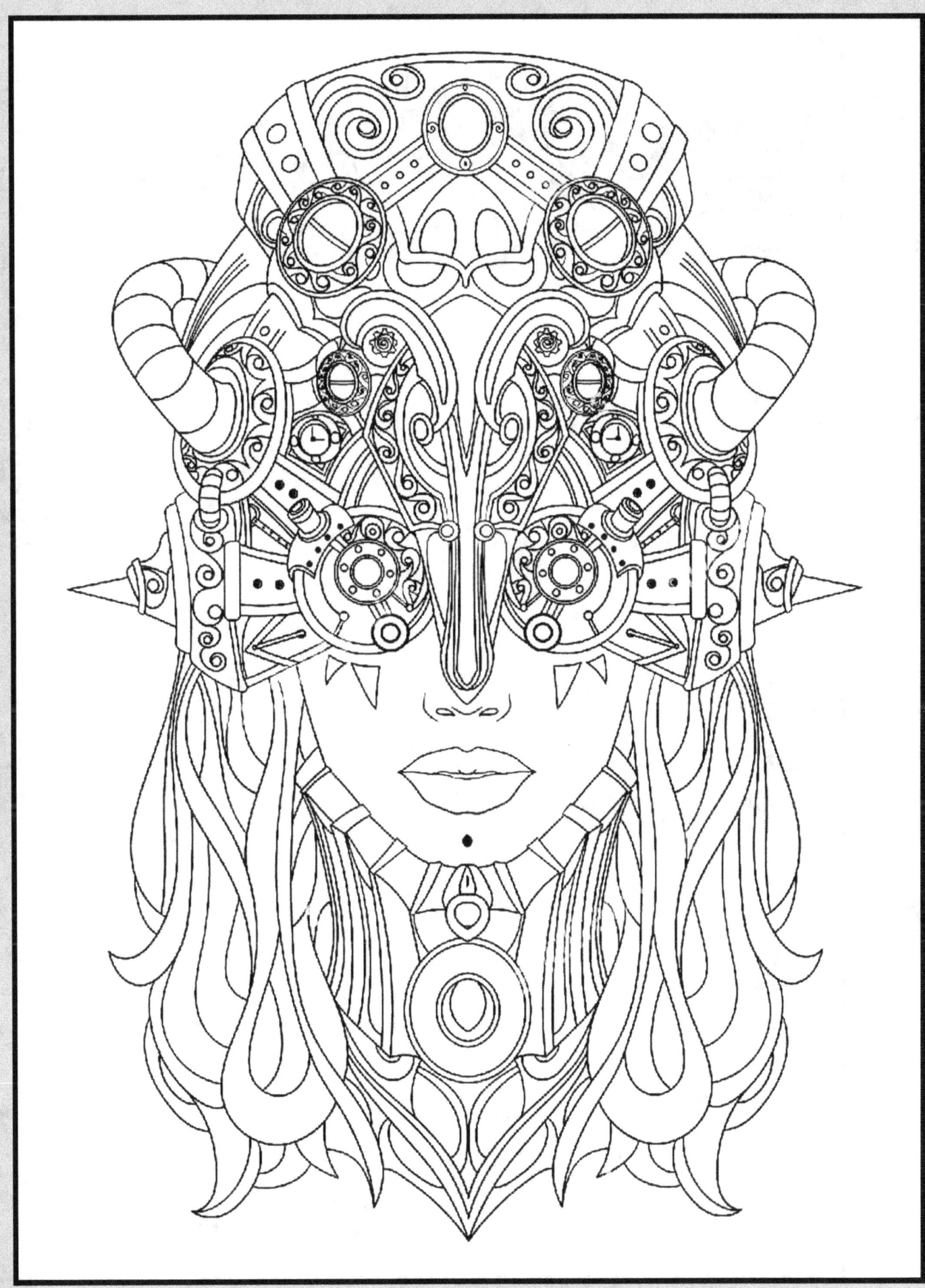

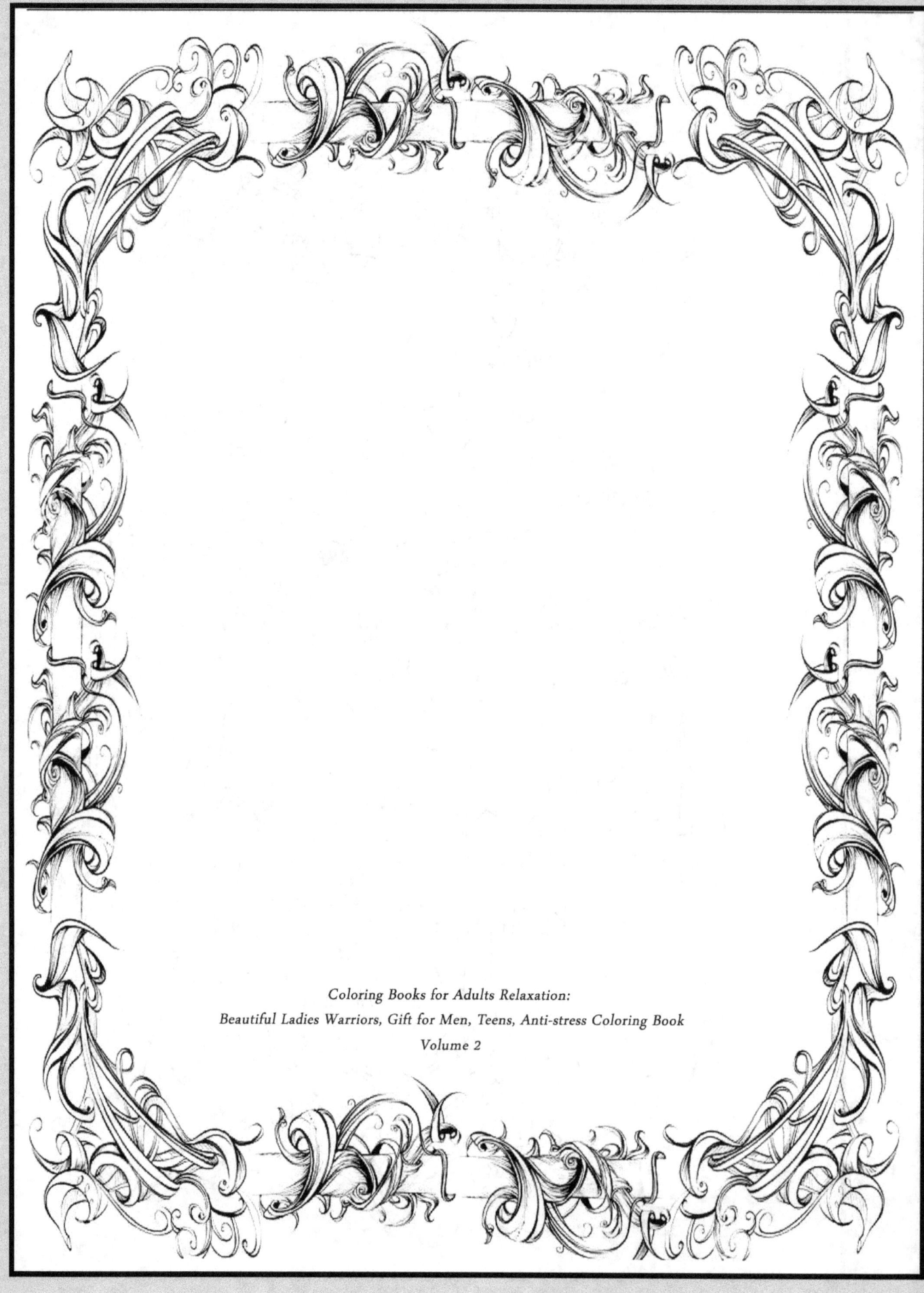

Coloring Books for Adults Relaxation:
Beautiful Ladies Warriors, Gift for Men, Teens, Anti-stress Coloring Book
Volume 2

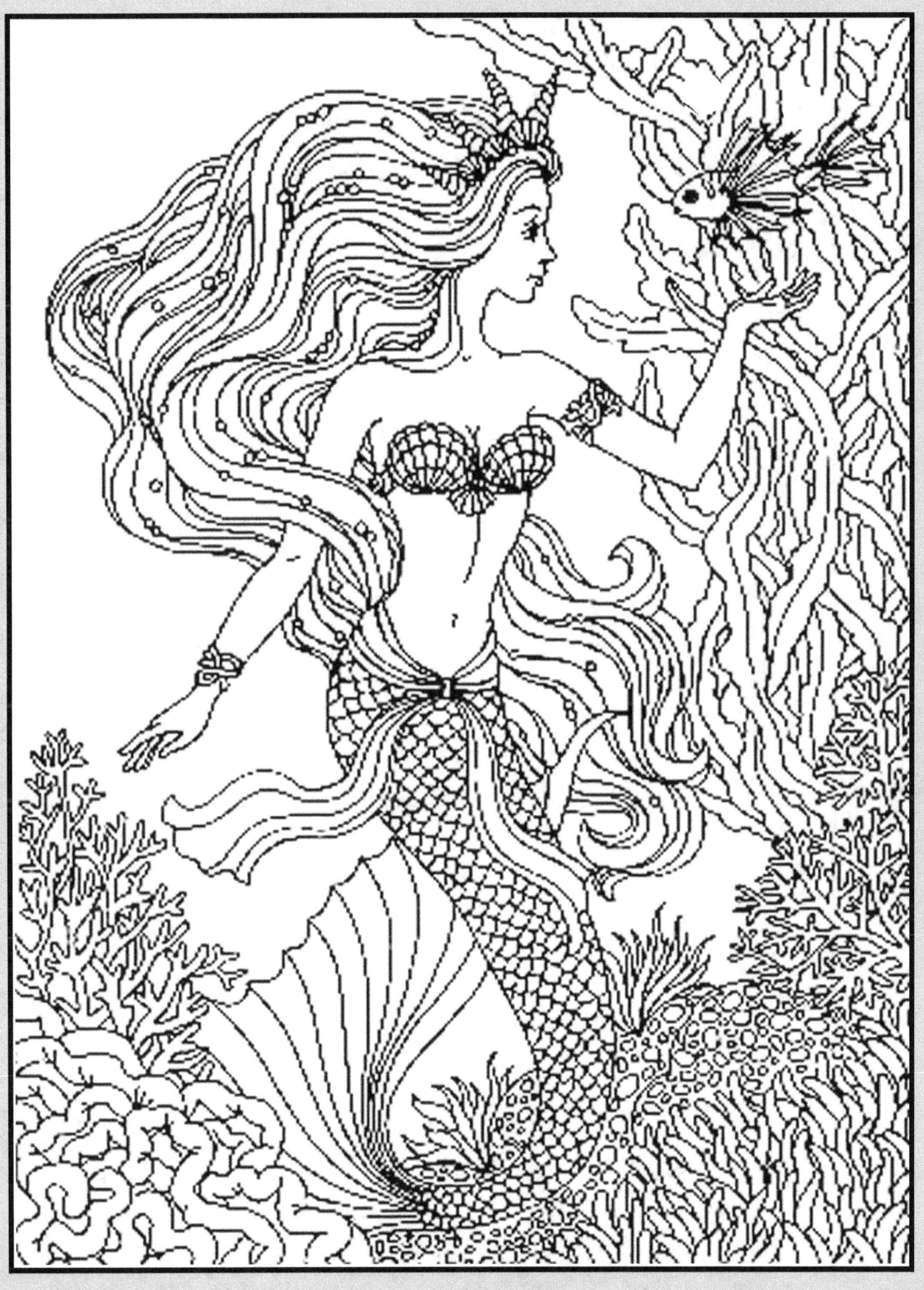

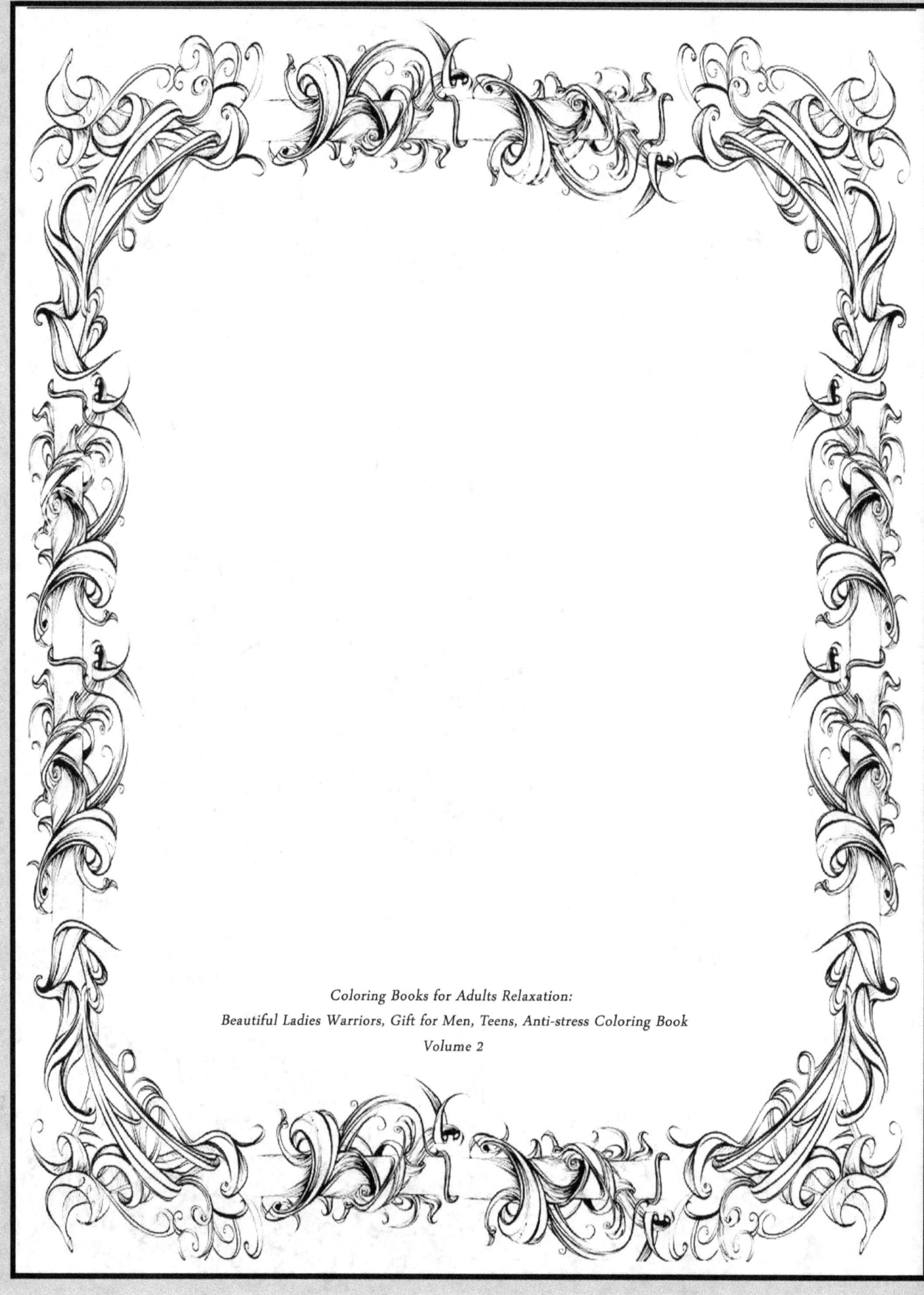

Coloring Books for Adults Relaxation:
Beautiful Ladies Warriors, Gift for Men, Teens, Anti-stress Coloring Book
Volume 2

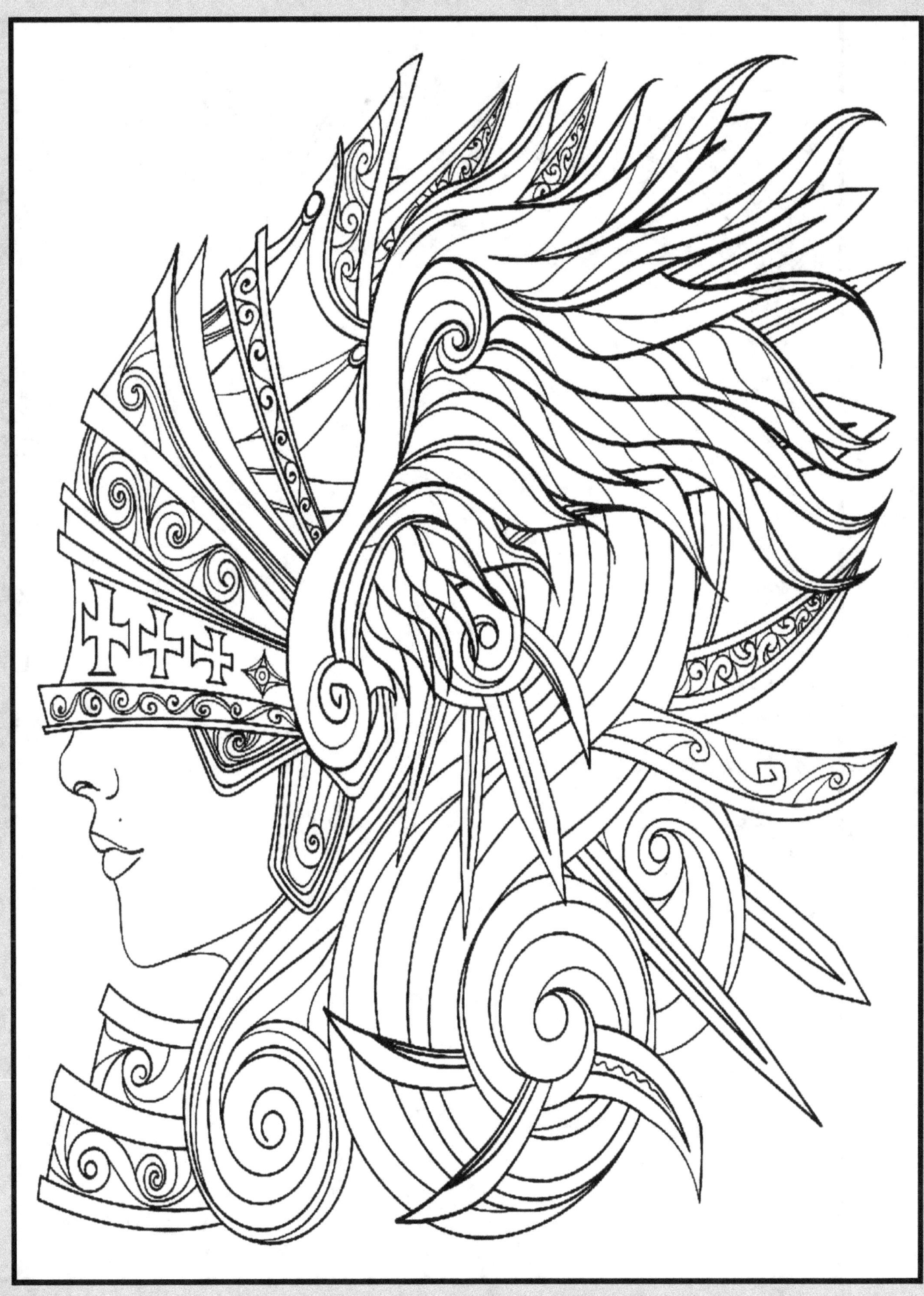

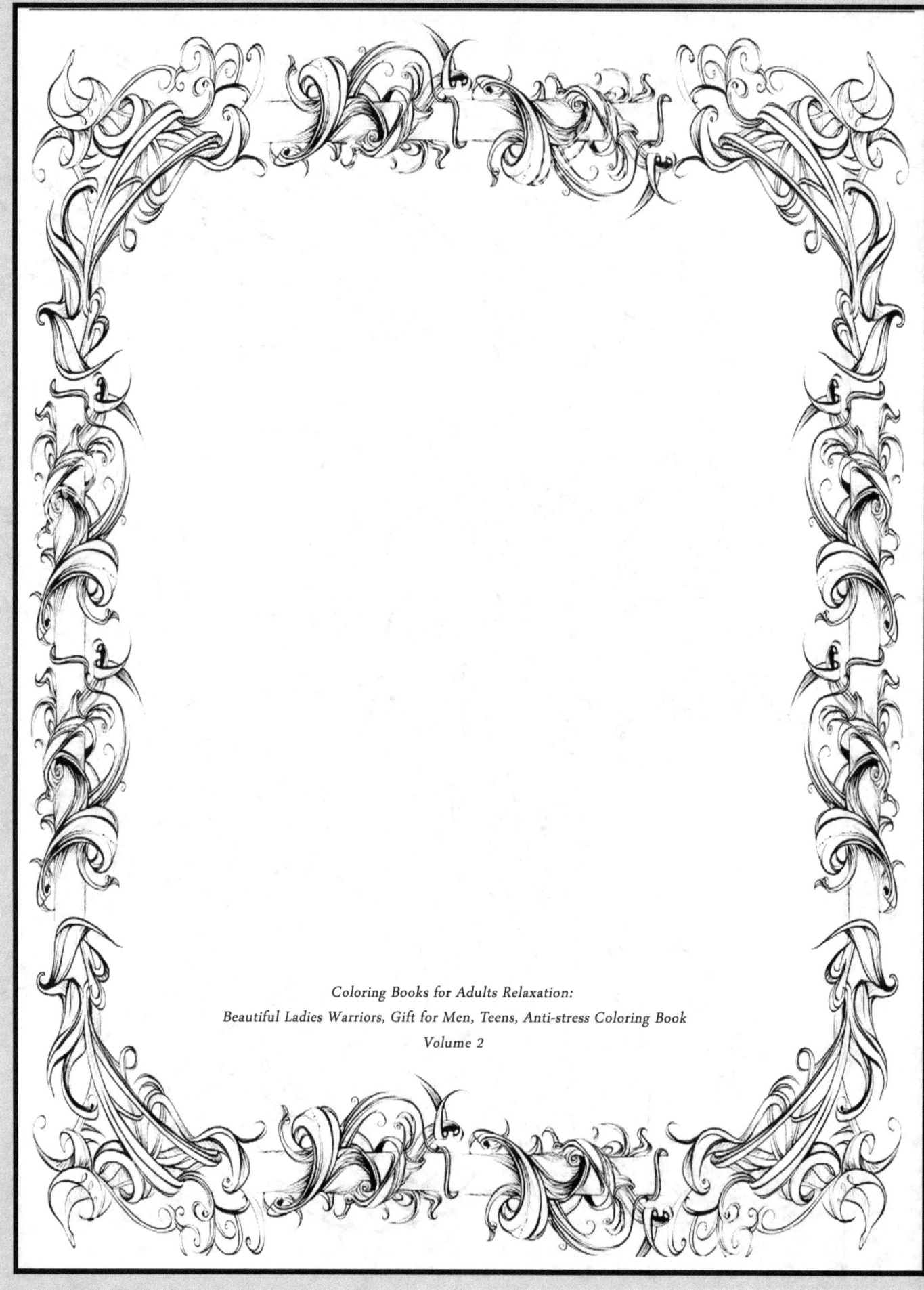

Coloring Books for Adults Relaxation:
Beautiful Ladies Warriors, Gift for Men, Teens, Anti-stress Coloring Book
Volume 2

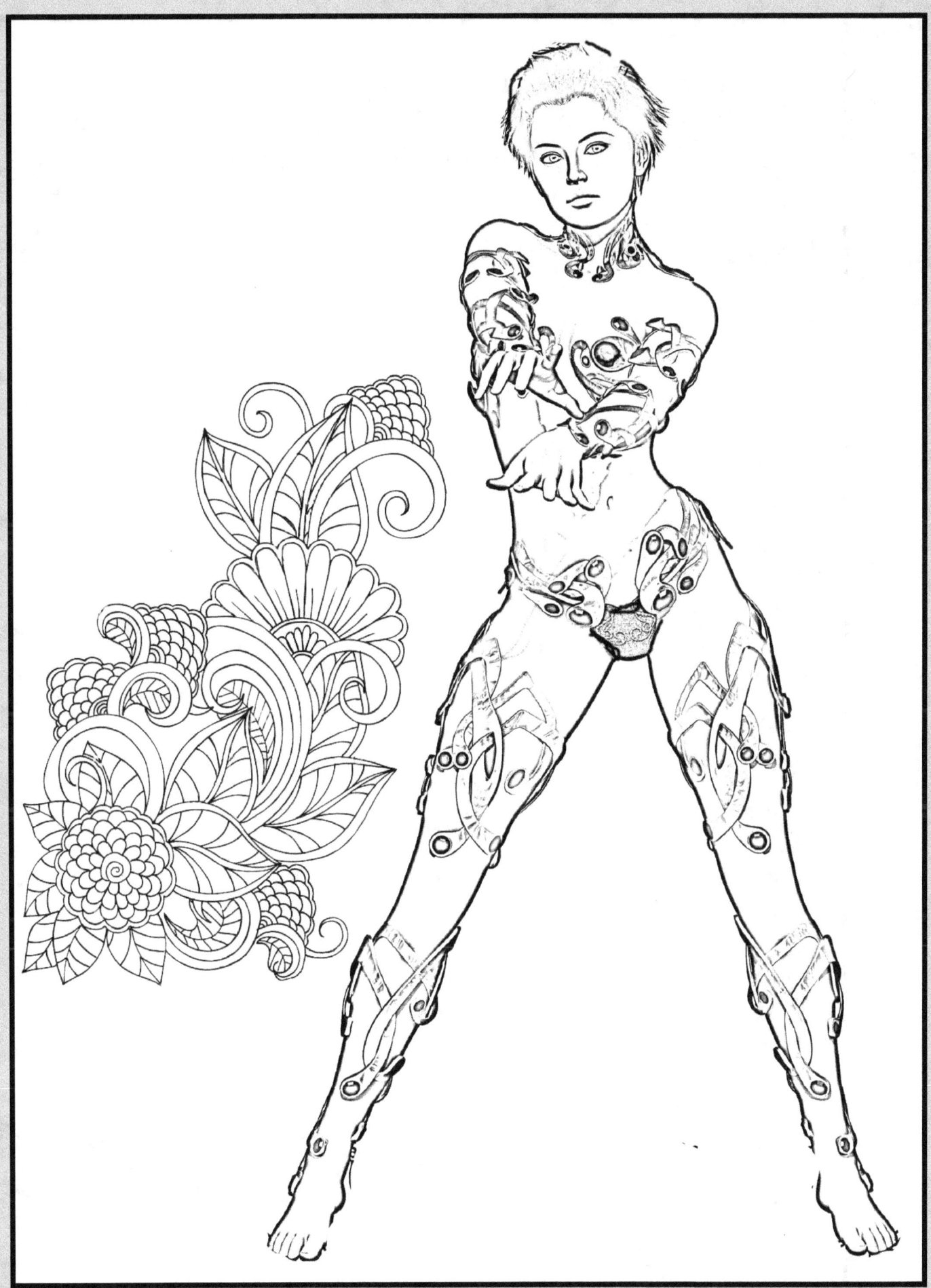

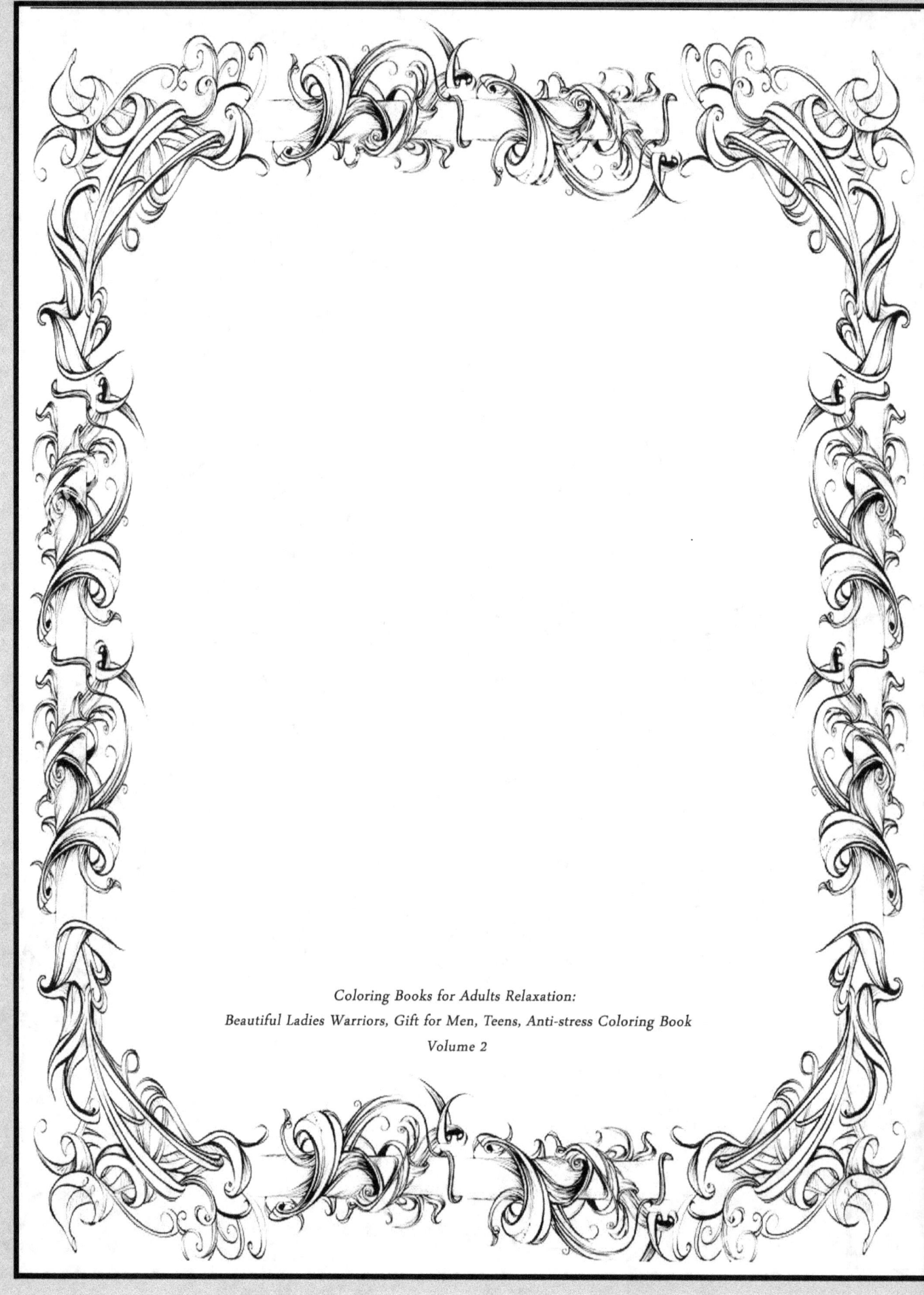

Coloring Books for Adults Relaxation:
Beautiful Ladies Warriors, Gift for Men, Teens, Anti-stress Coloring Book
Volume 2

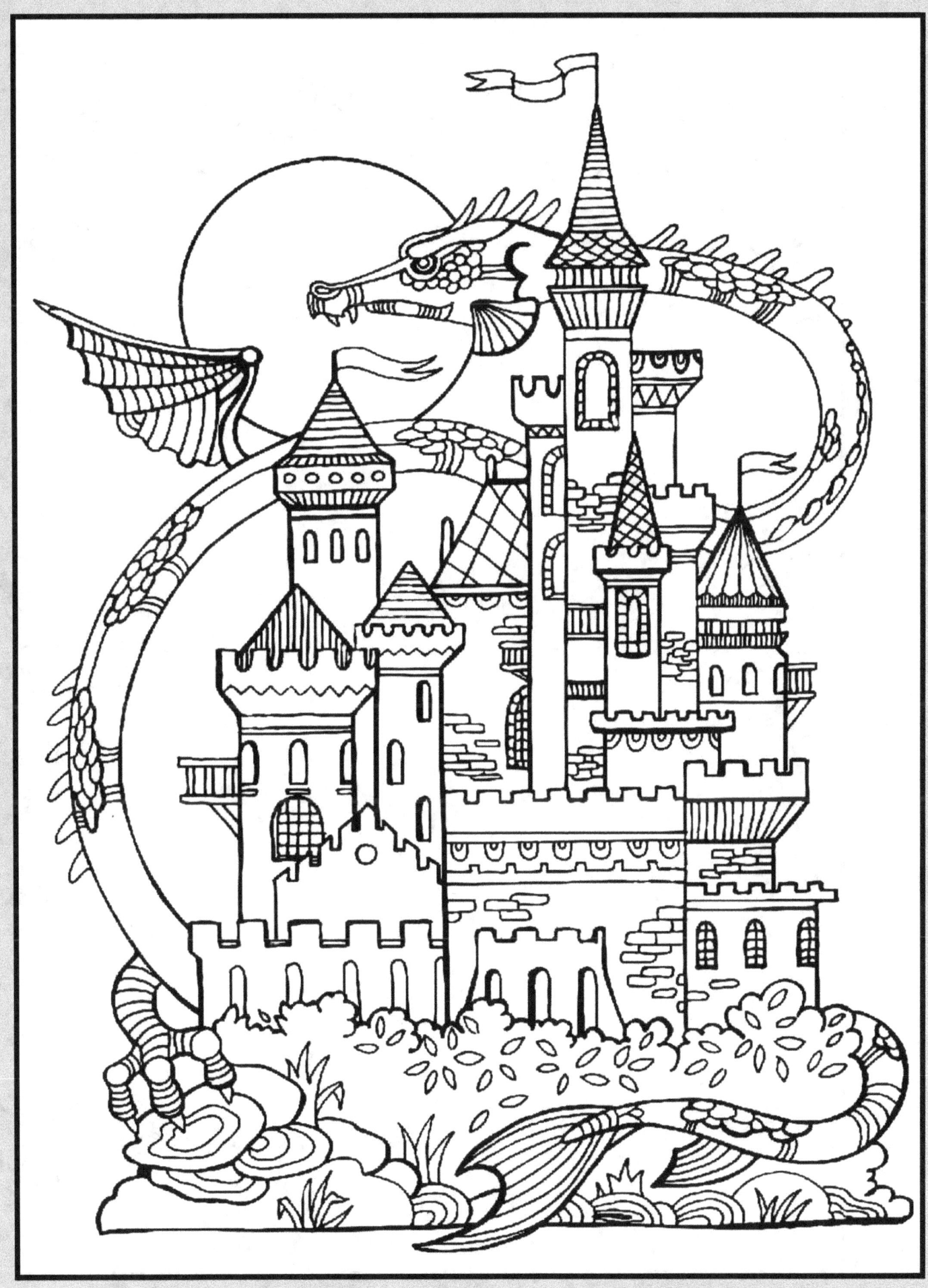

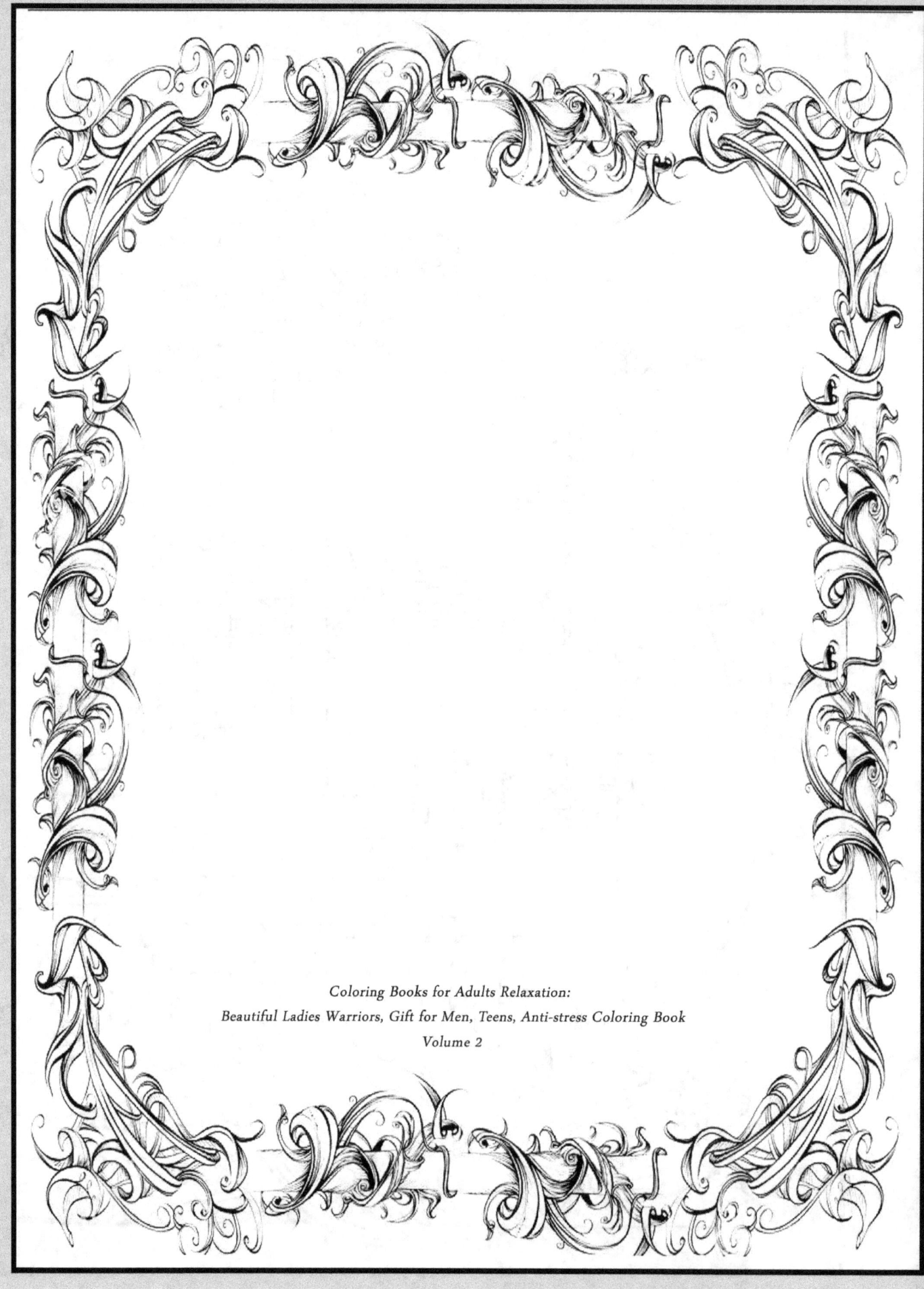

Coloring Books for Adults Relaxation:
Beautiful Ladies Warriors, Gift for Men, Teens, Anti-stress Coloring Book
Volume 2

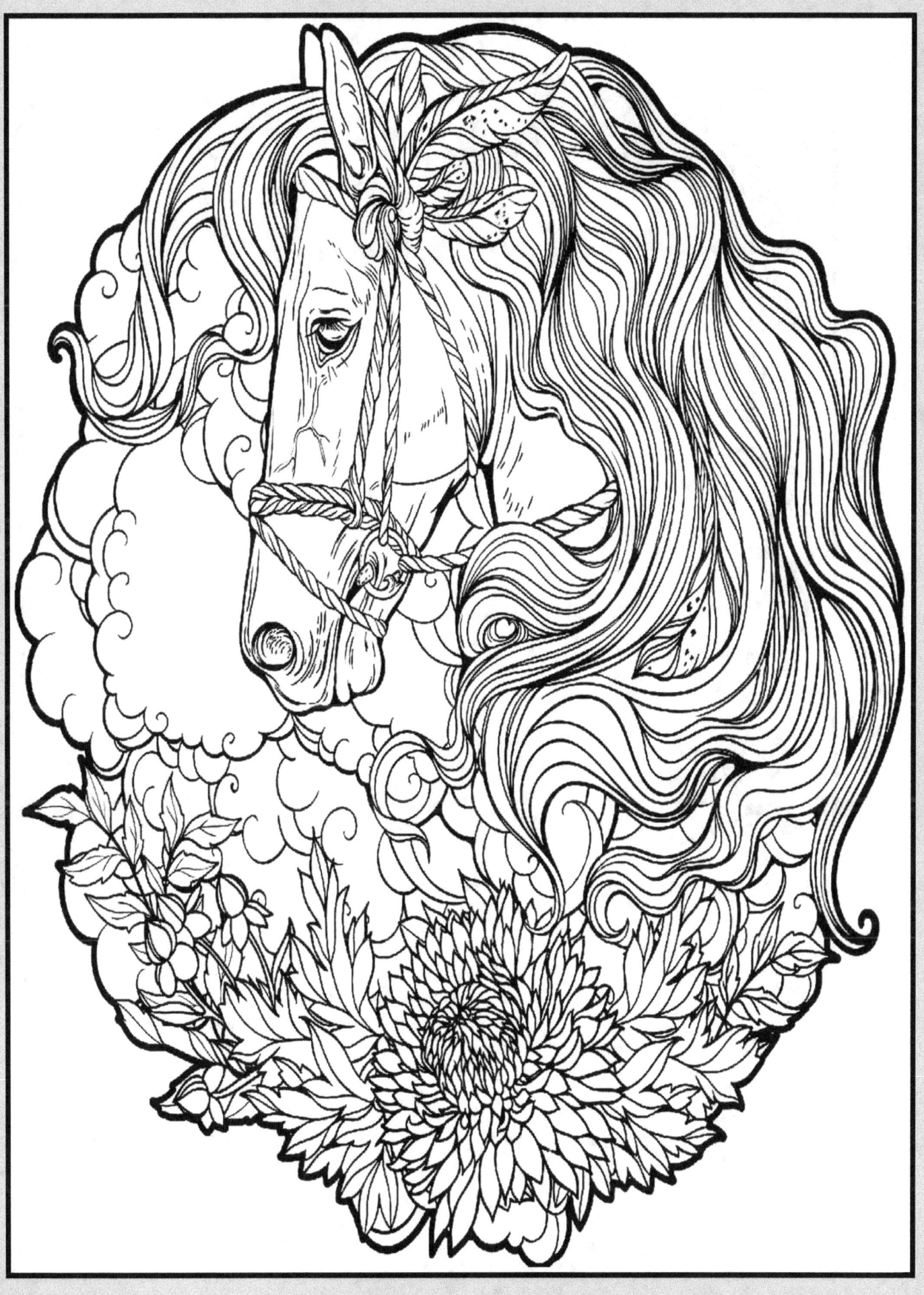

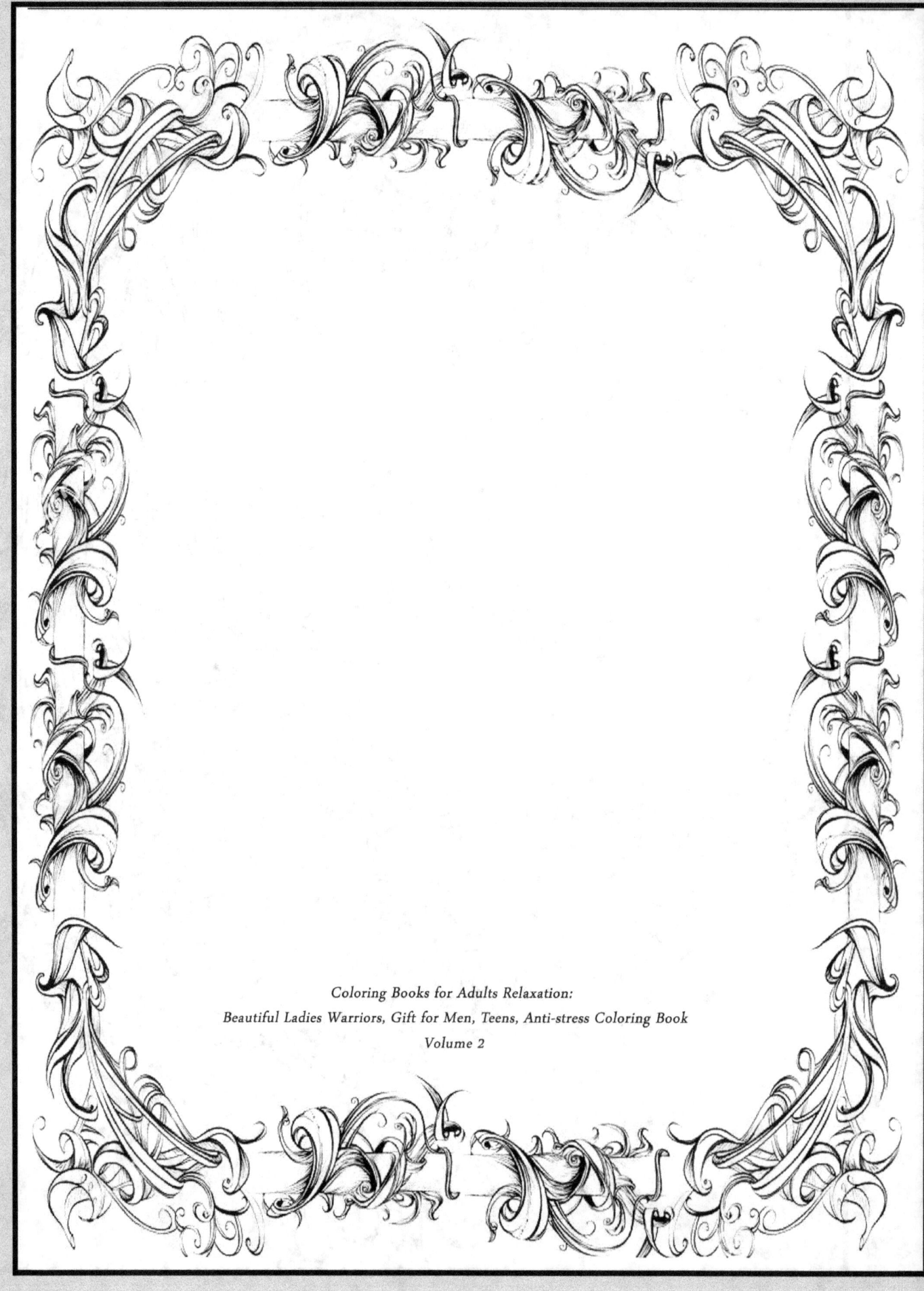

Coloring Books for Adults Relaxation:
Beautiful Ladies Warriors, Gift for Men, Teens, Anti-stress Coloring Book
Volume 2

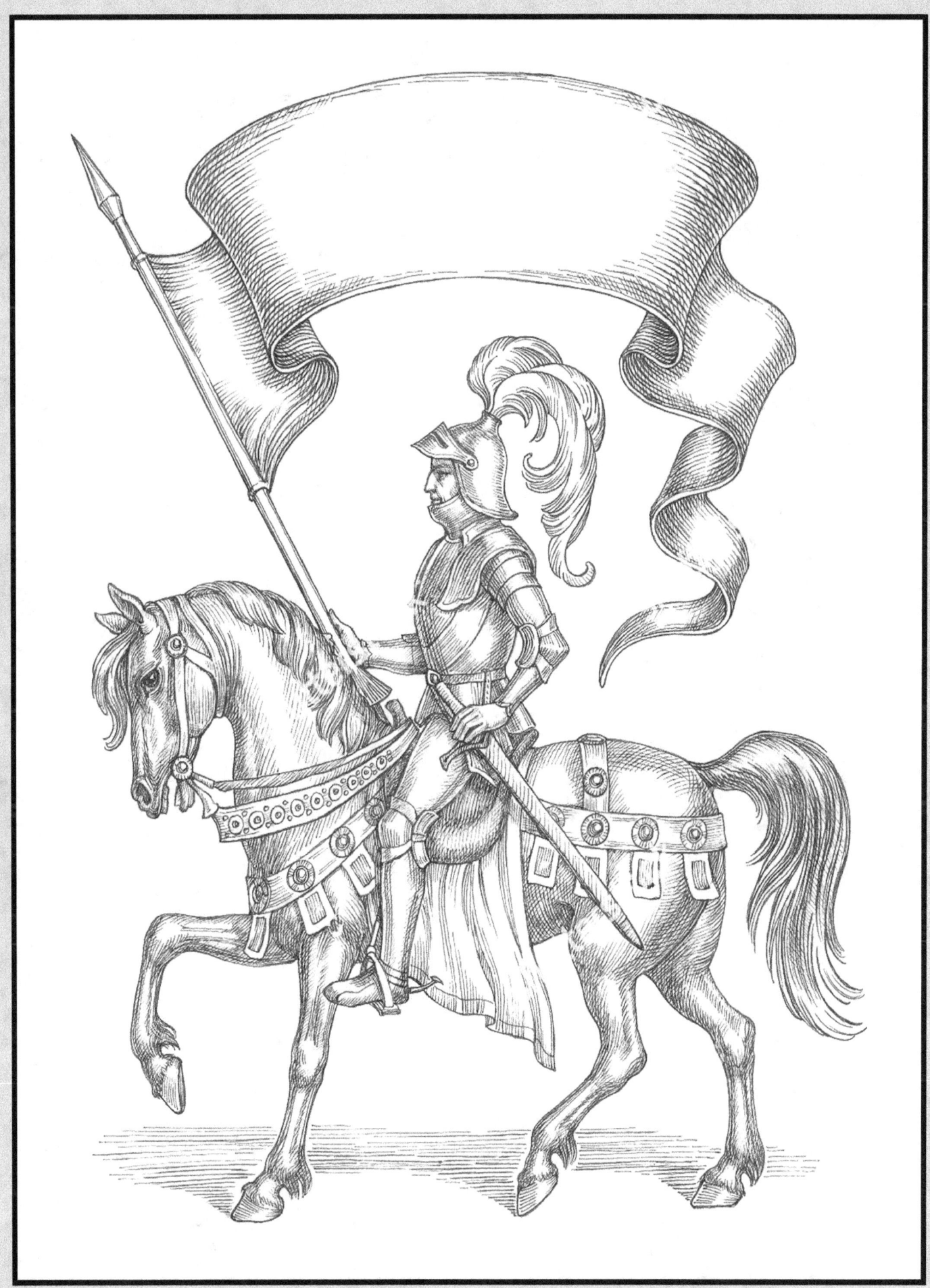

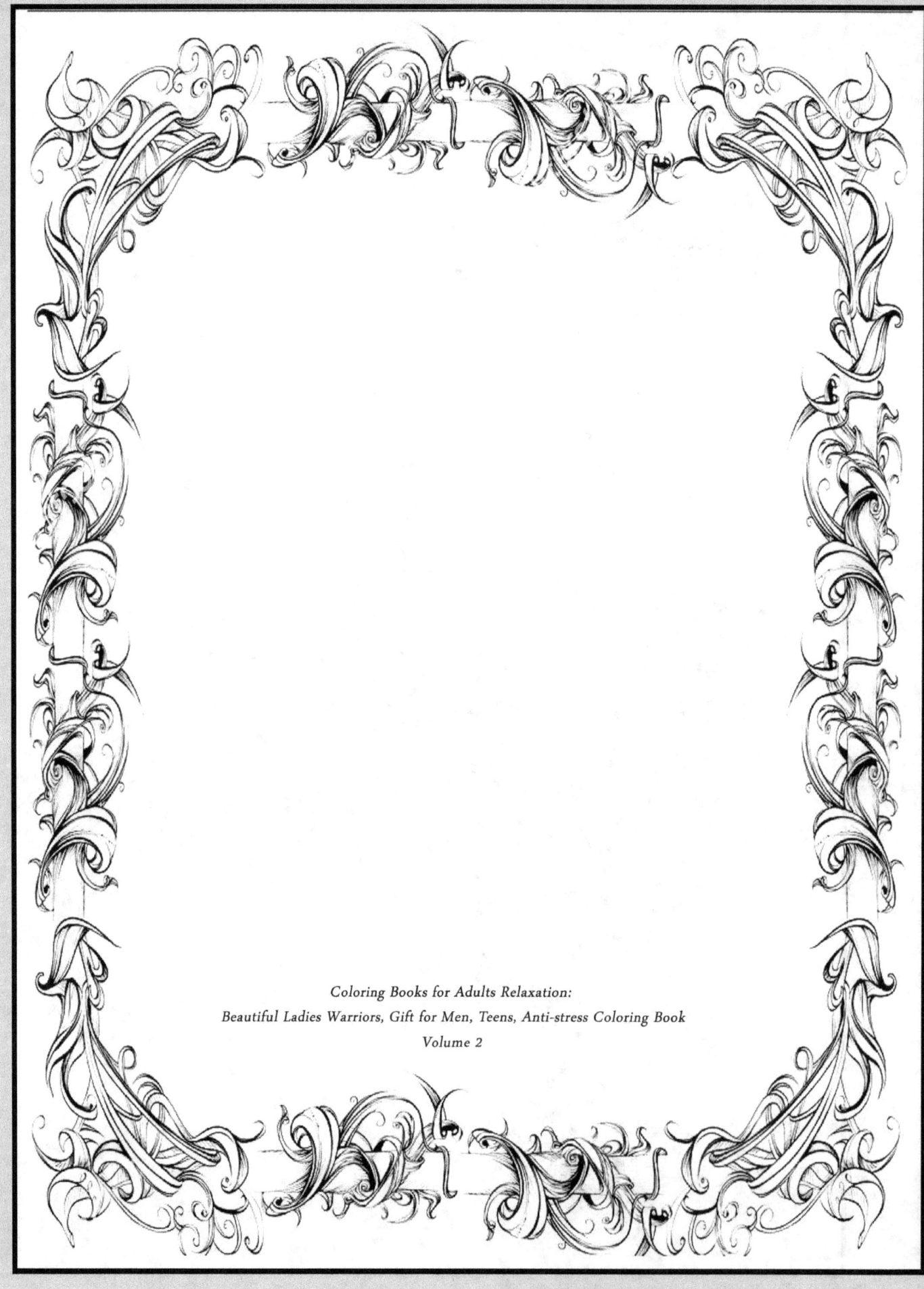

Coloring Books for Adults Relaxation:
Beautiful Ladies Warriors, Gift for Men, Teens, Anti-stress Coloring Book
Volume 2

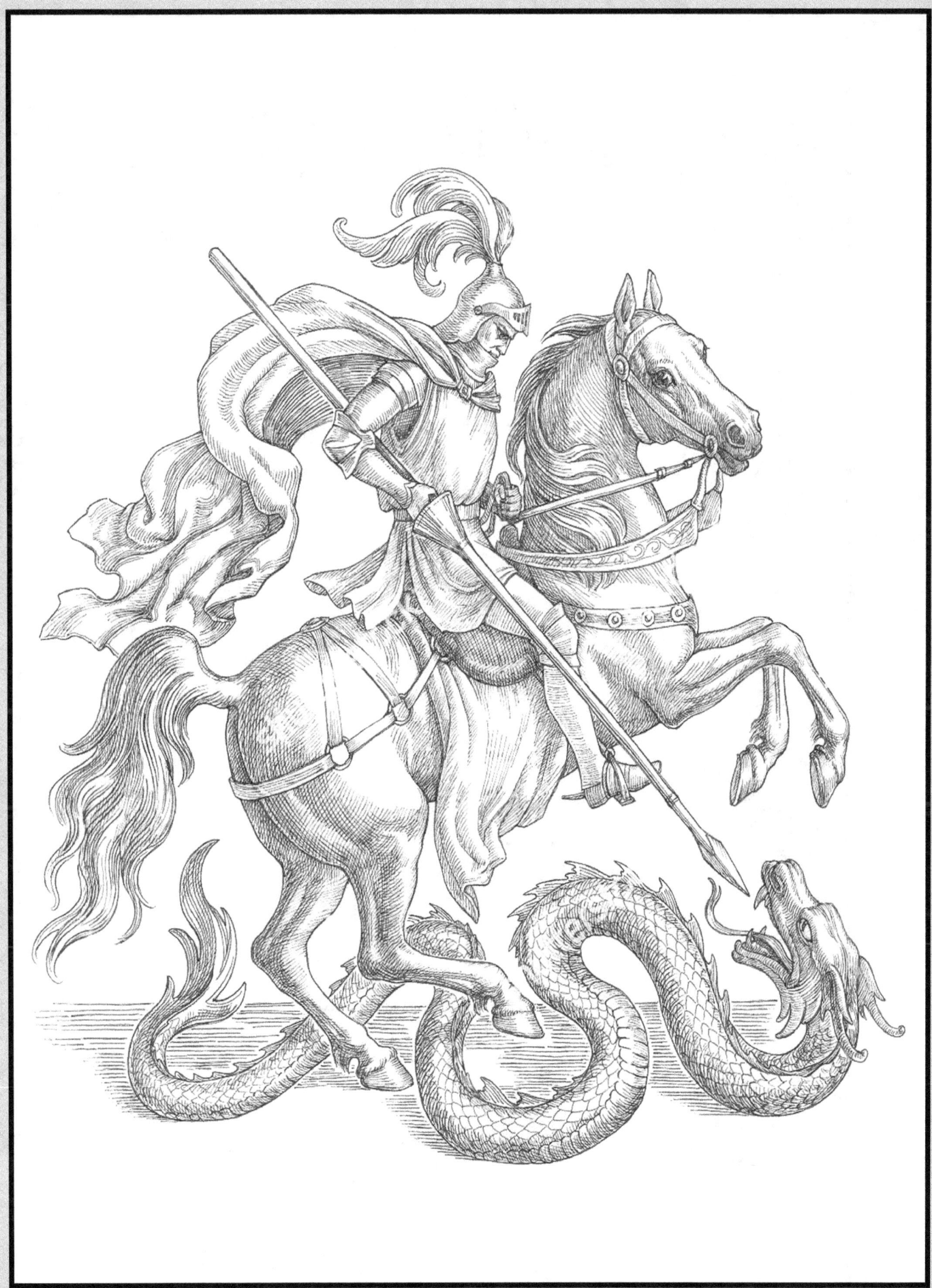

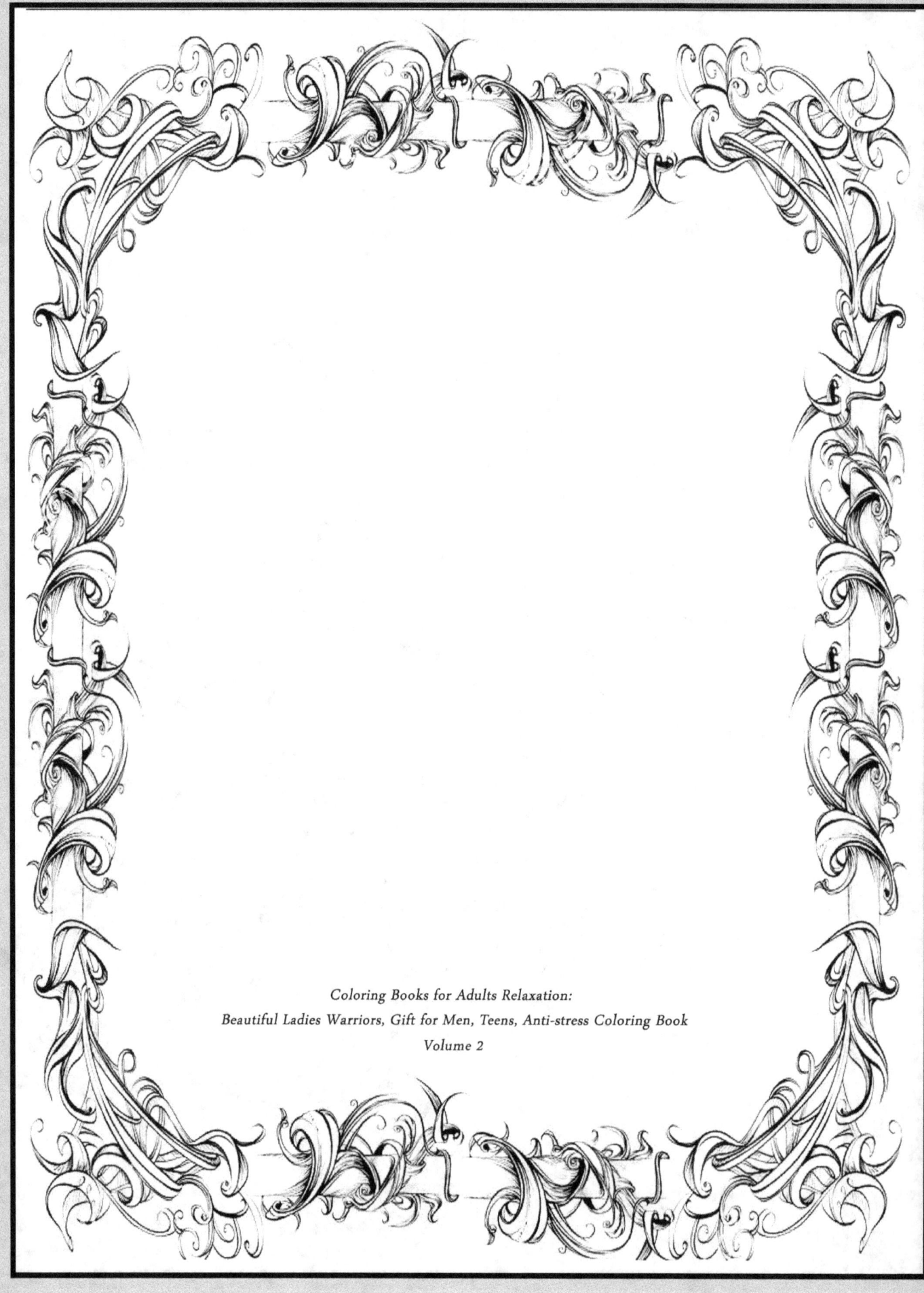

Coloring Books for Adults Relaxation:
Beautiful Ladies Warriors, Gift for Men, Teens, Anti-stress Coloring Book
Volume 2

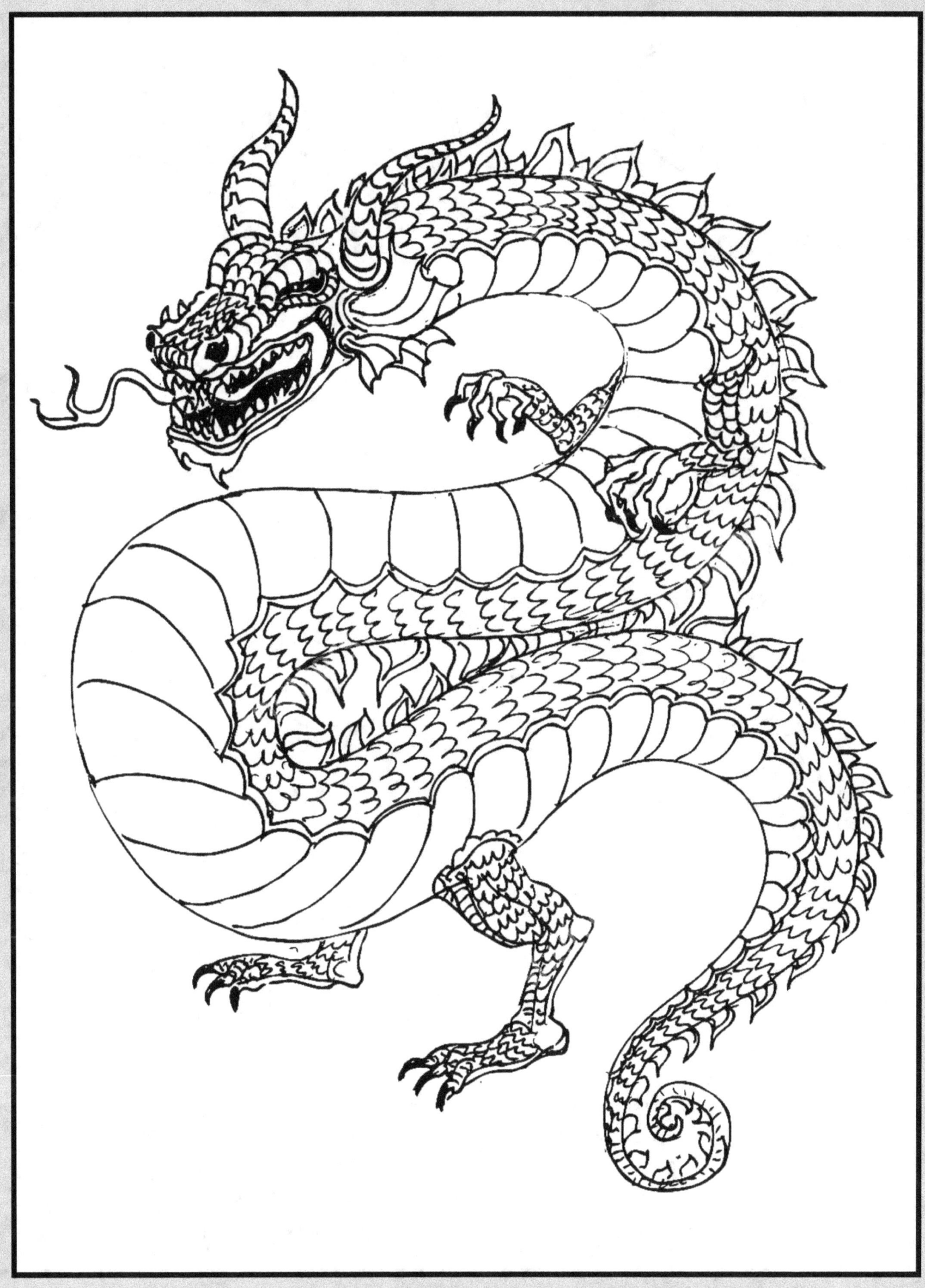

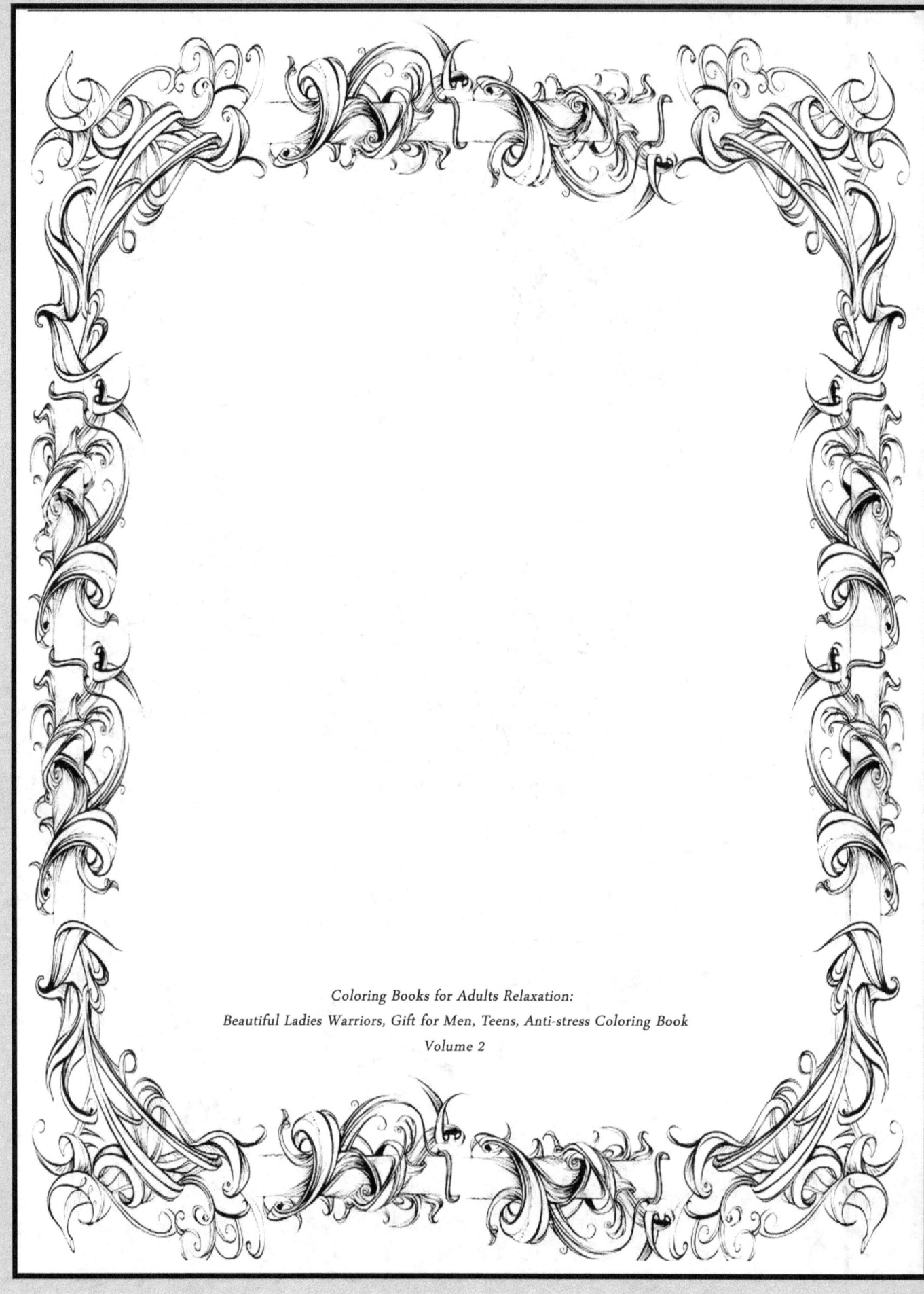

Coloring Books for Adults Relaxation:
Beautiful Ladies Warriors, Gift for Men, Teens, Anti-stress Coloring Book
Volume 2

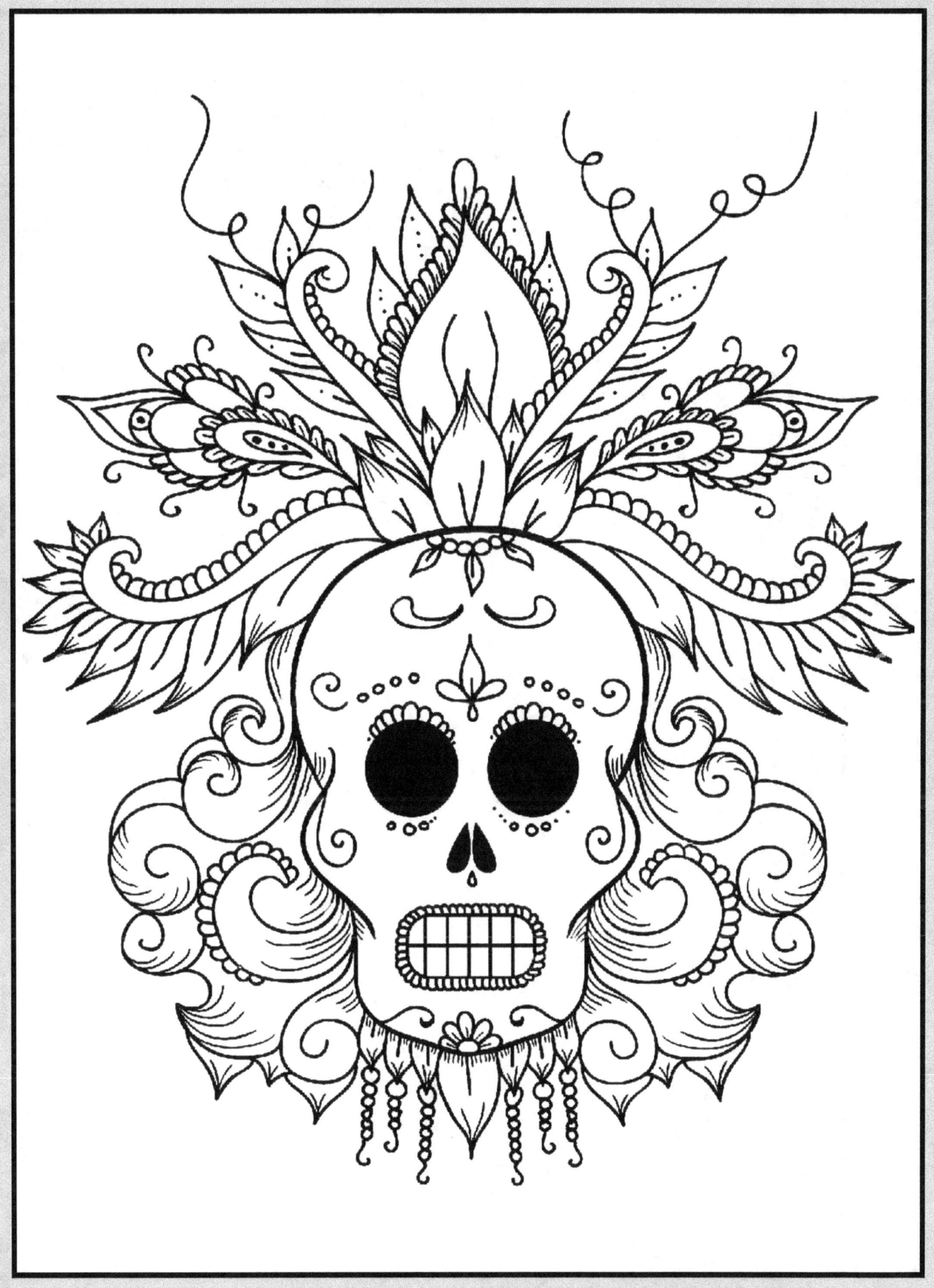

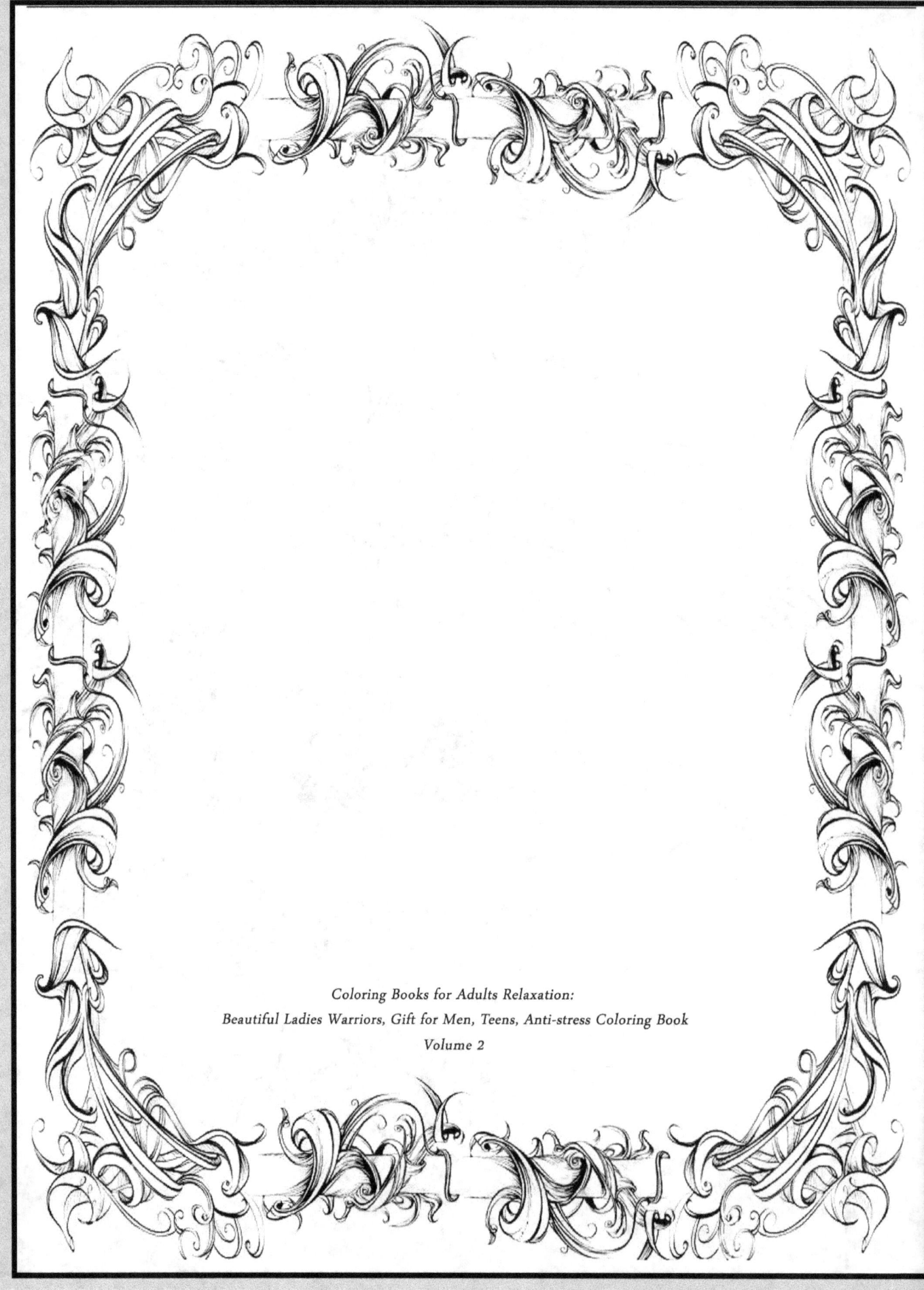

Coloring Books for Adults Relaxation:
Beautiful Ladies Warriors, Gift for Men, Teens, Anti-stress Coloring Book
Volume 2

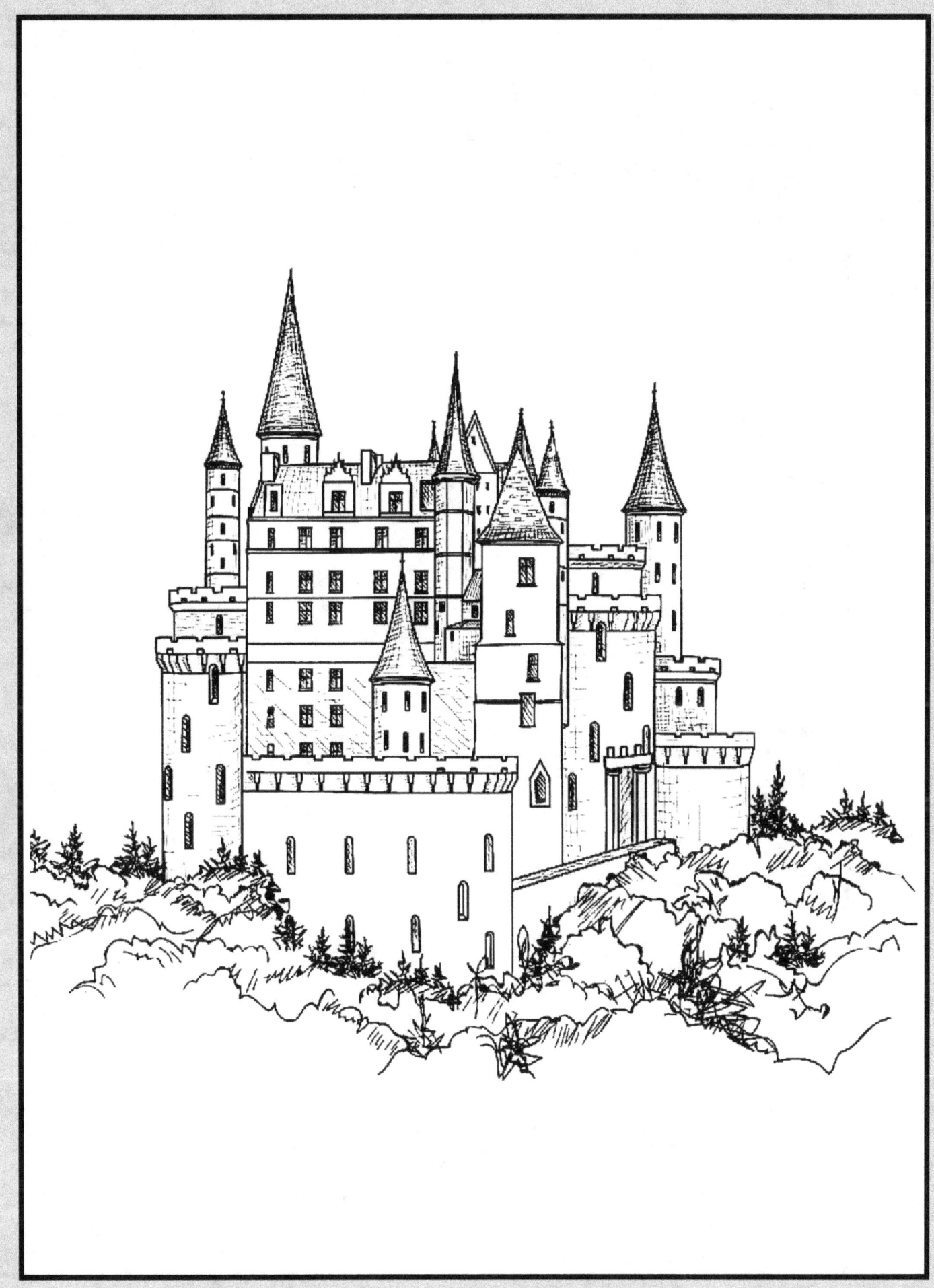

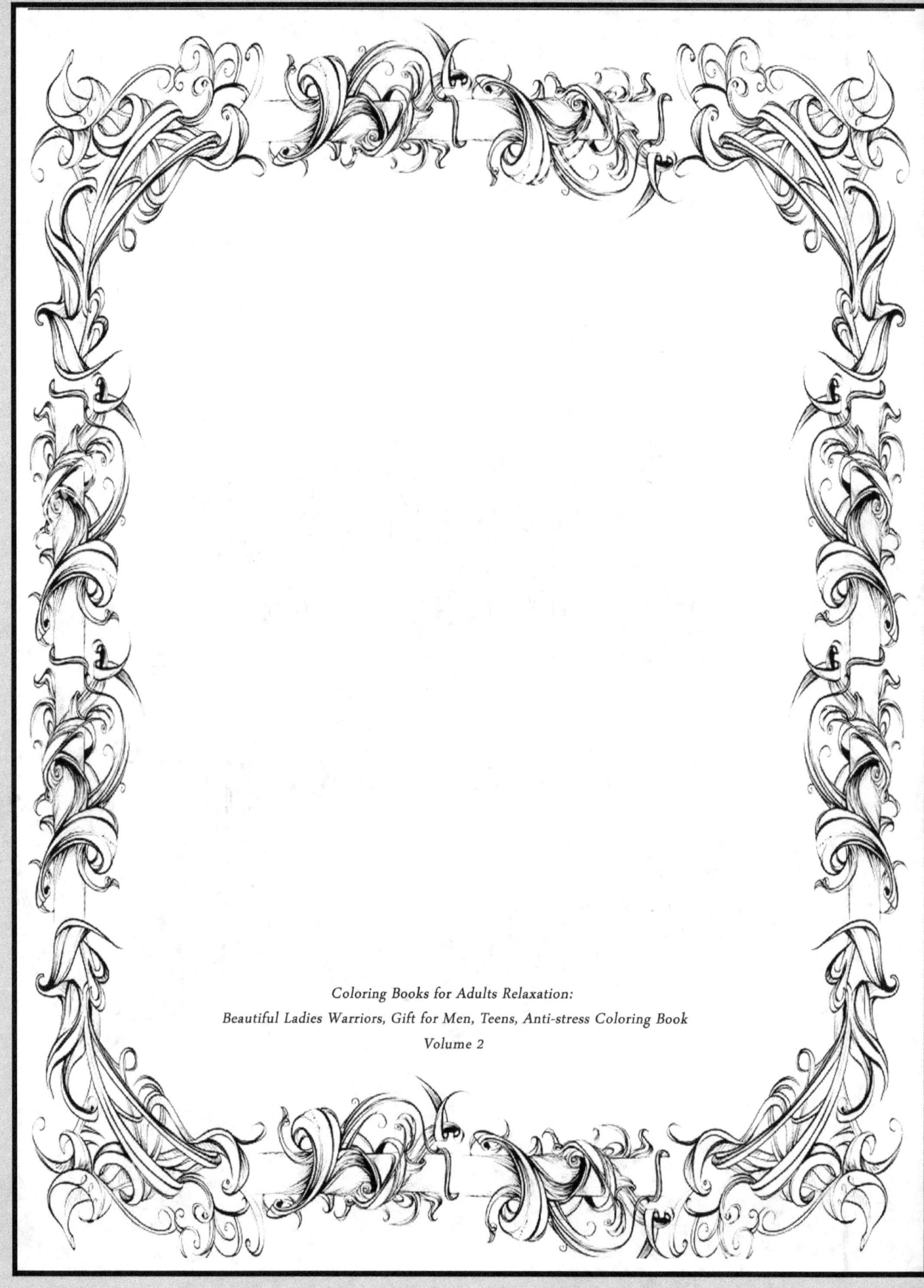

Coloring Books for Adults Relaxation:
Beautiful Ladies Warriors, Gift for Men, Teens, Anti-stress Coloring Book
Volume 2

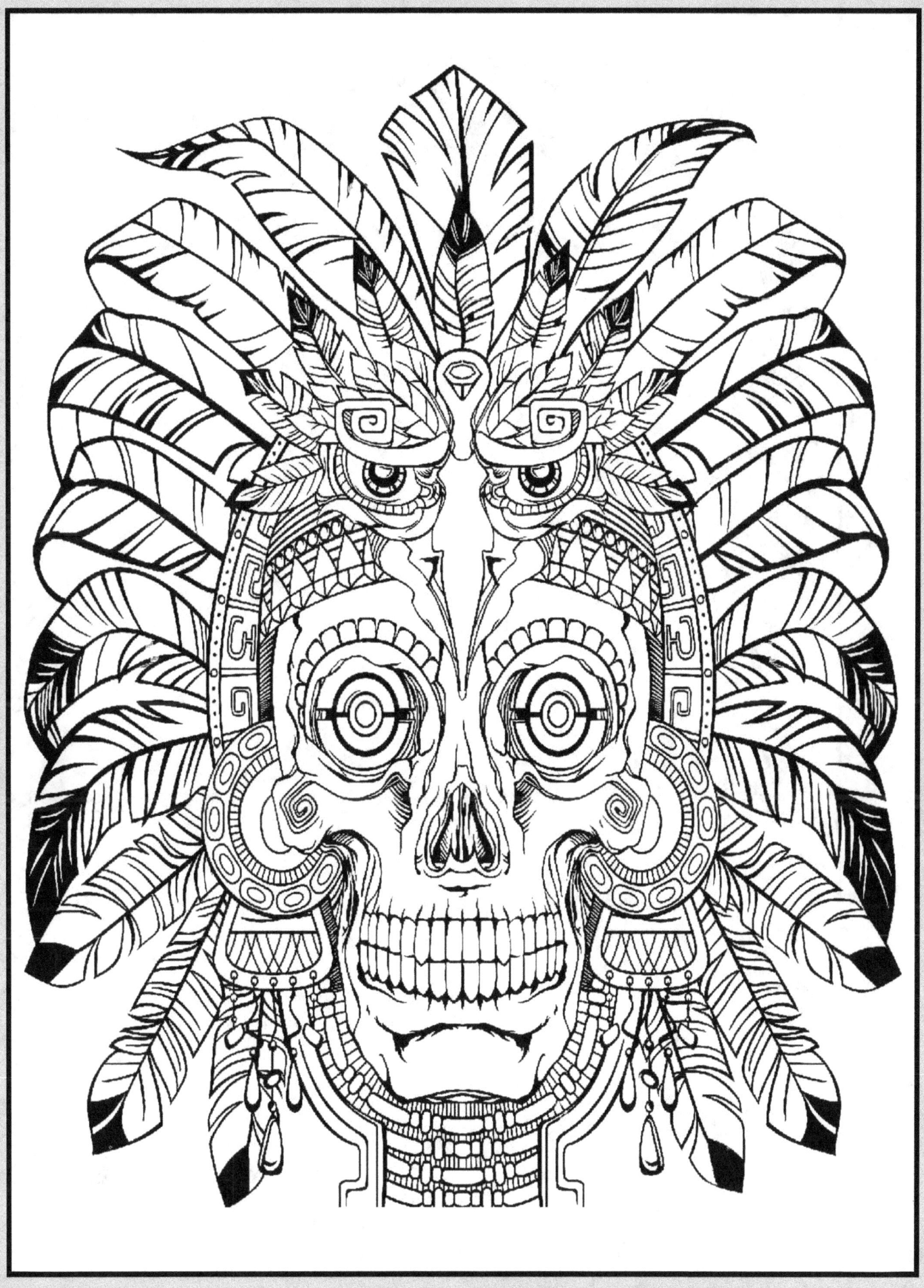

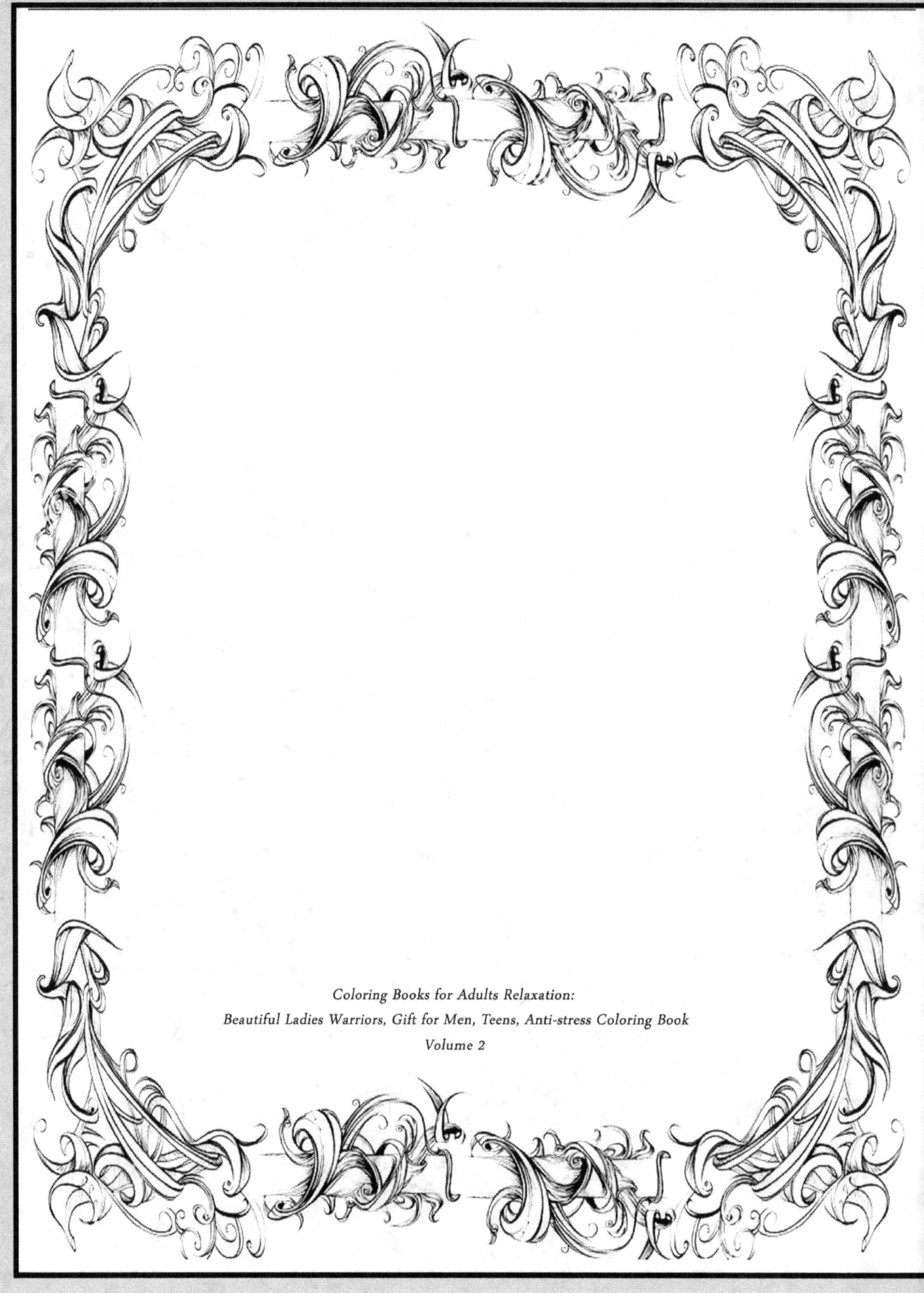

Coloring Books for Adults Relaxation:
Beautiful Ladies Warriors, Gift for Men, Teens, Anti-stress Coloring Book
Volume 2

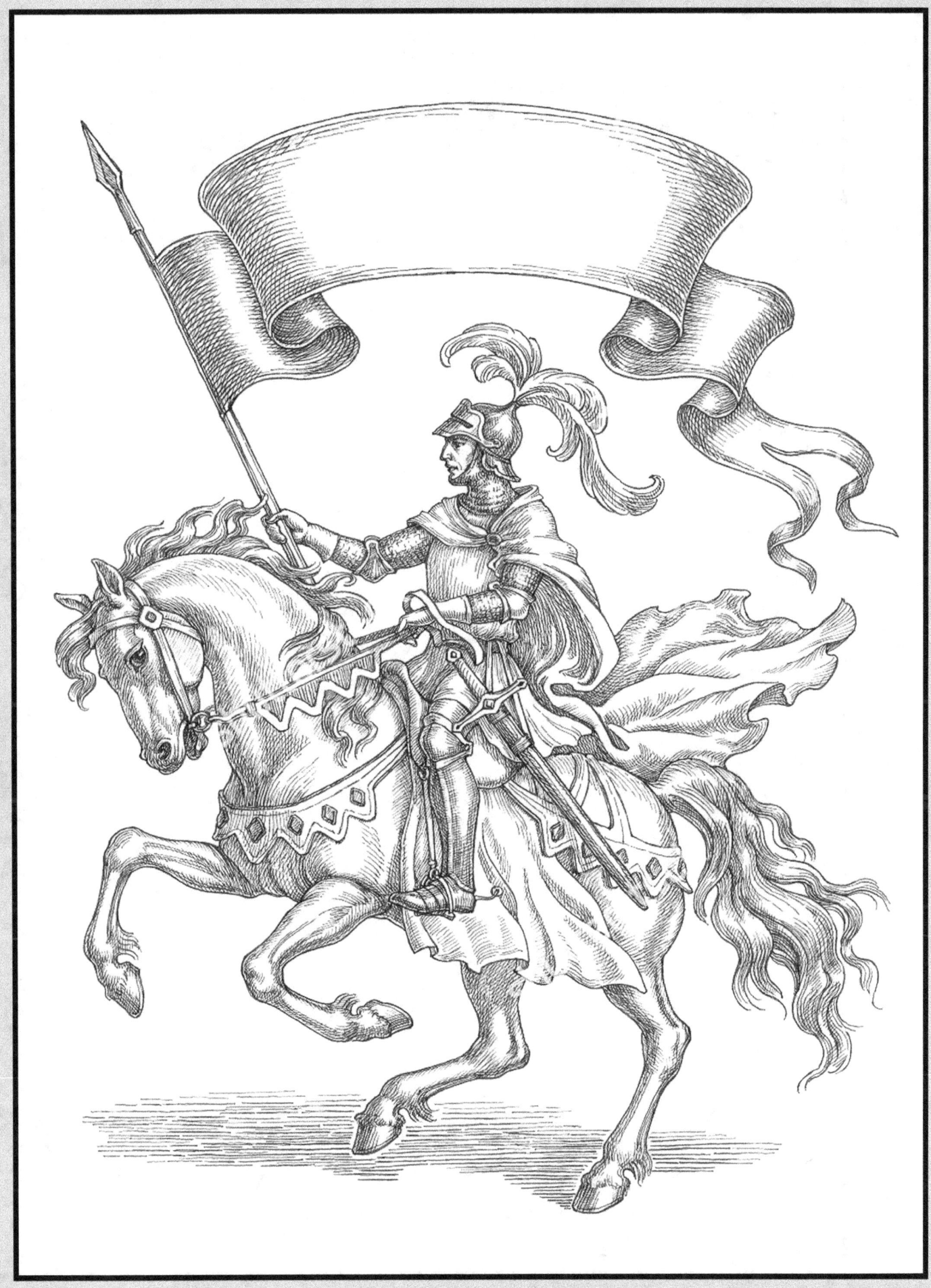

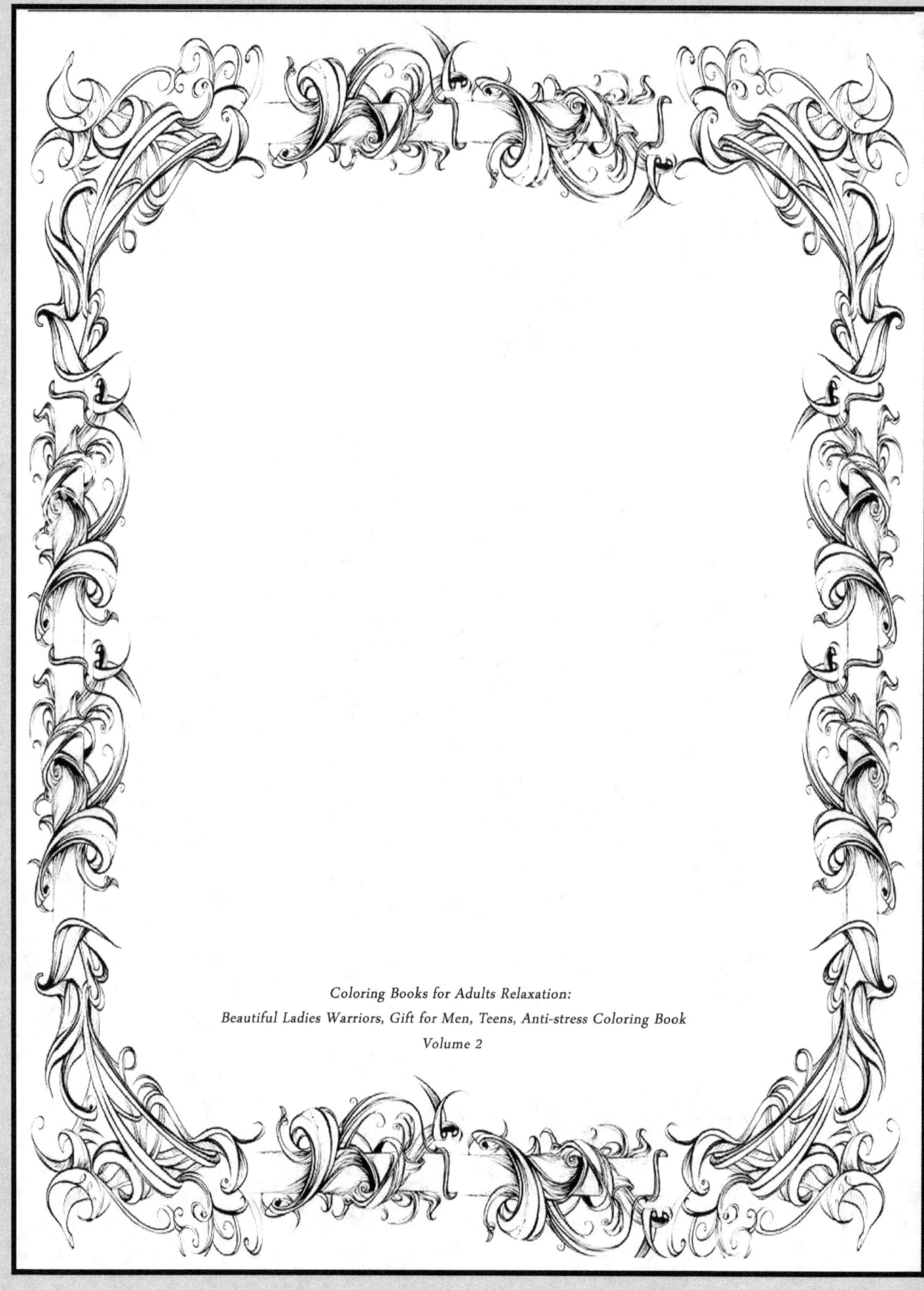

Coloring Books for Adults Relaxation:
Beautiful Ladies Warriors, Gift for Men, Teens, Anti-stress Coloring Book
Volume 2

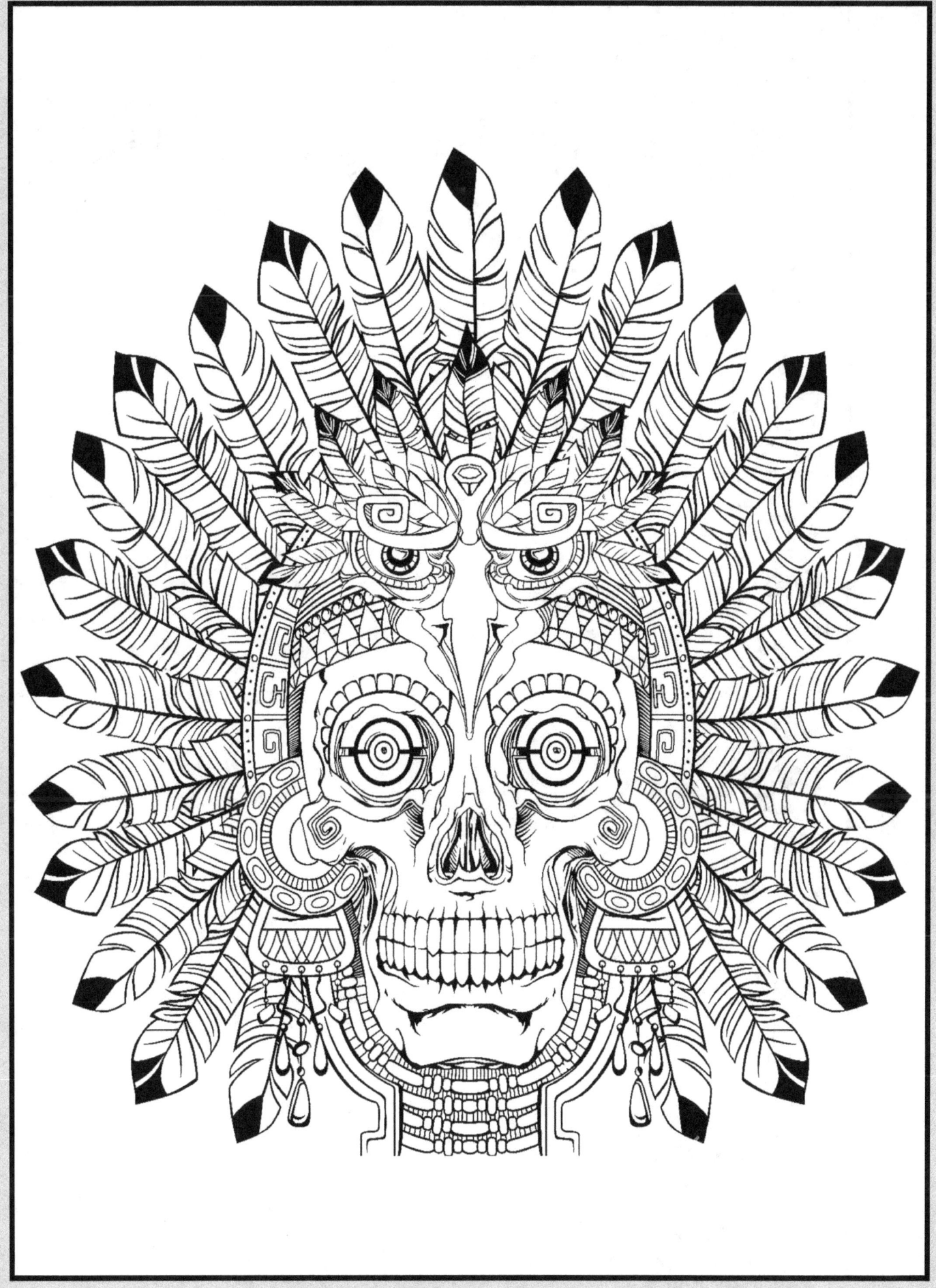

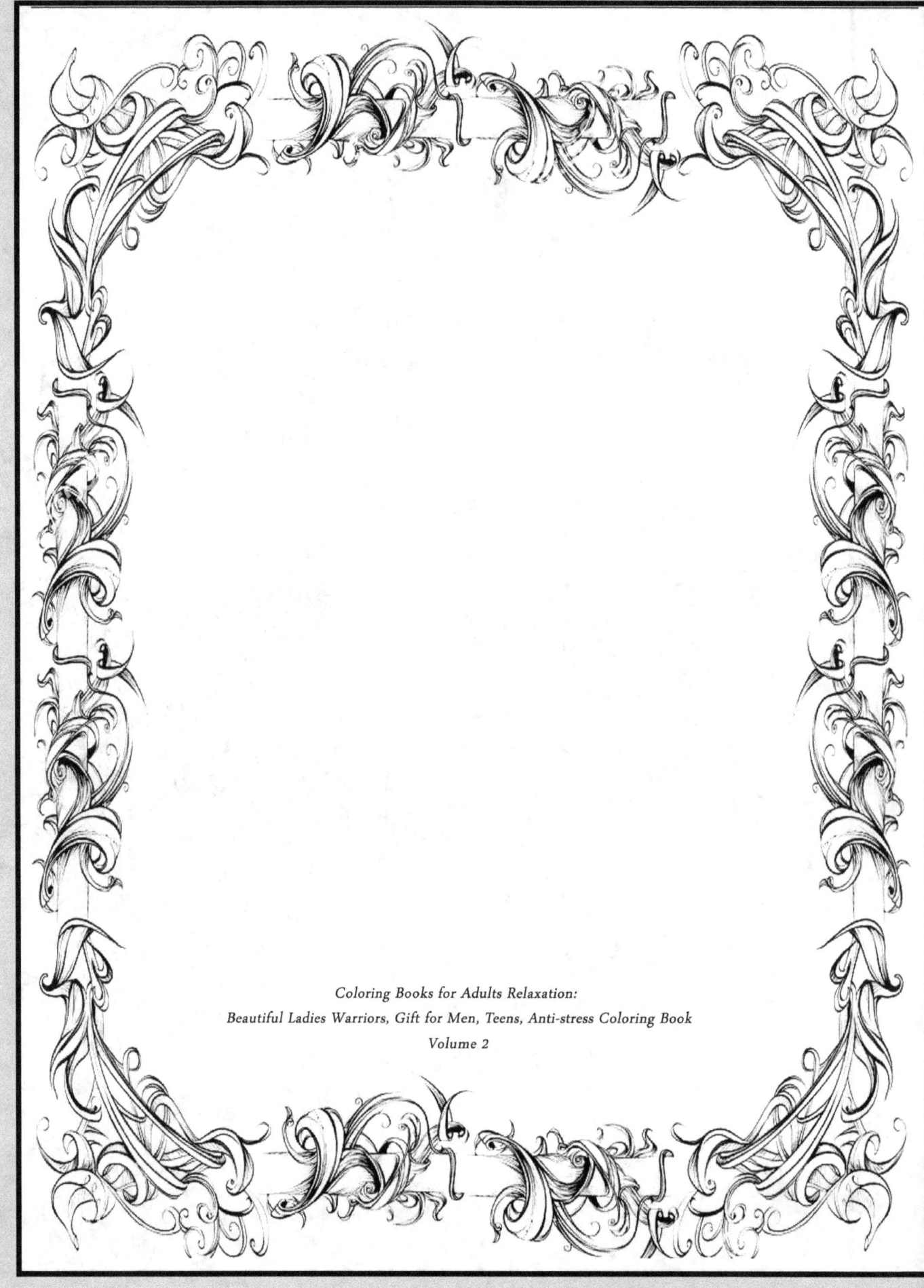

Coloring Books for Adults Relaxation:
Beautiful Ladies Warriors, Gift for Men, Teens, Anti-stress Coloring Book
Volume 2

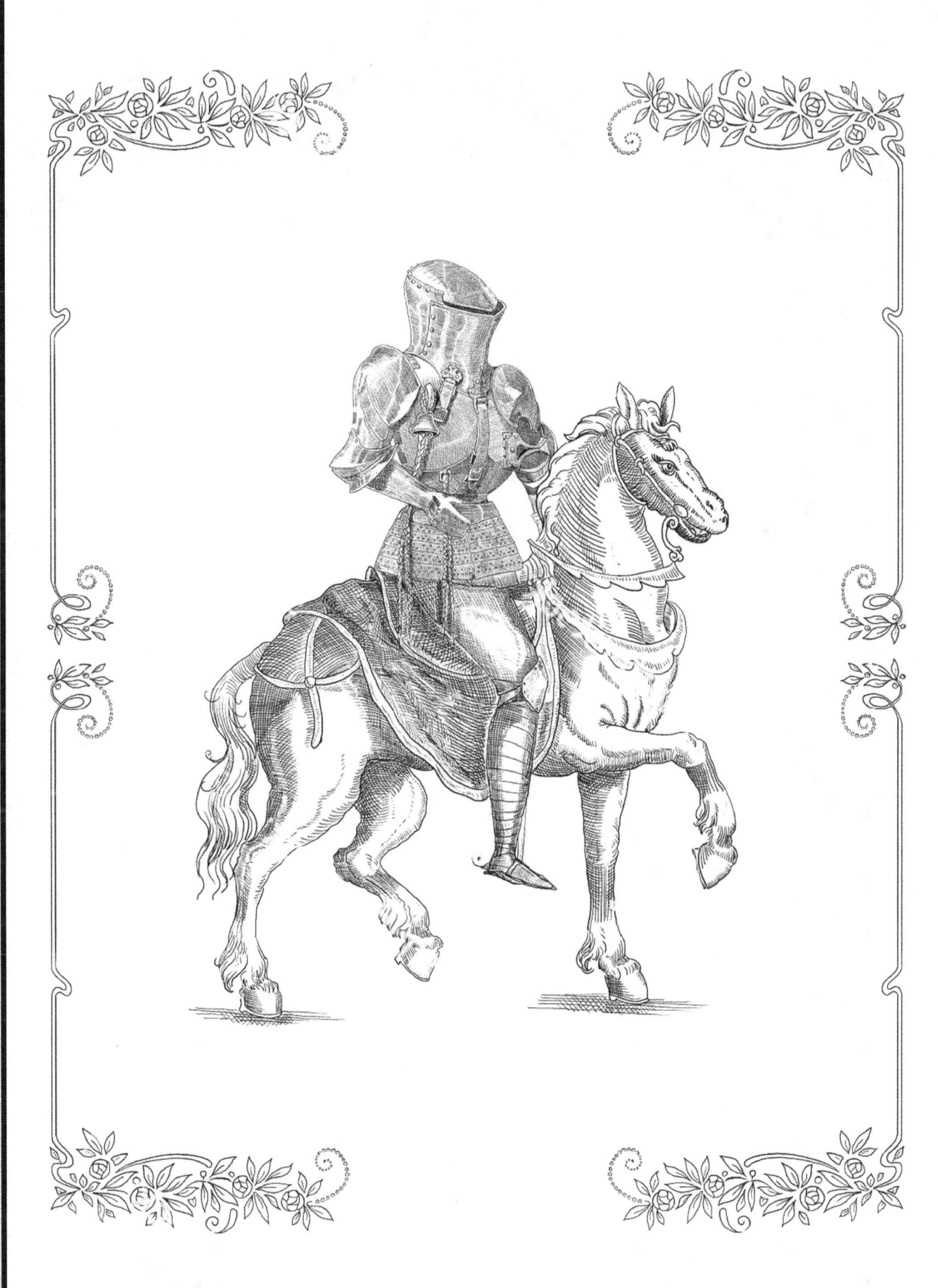

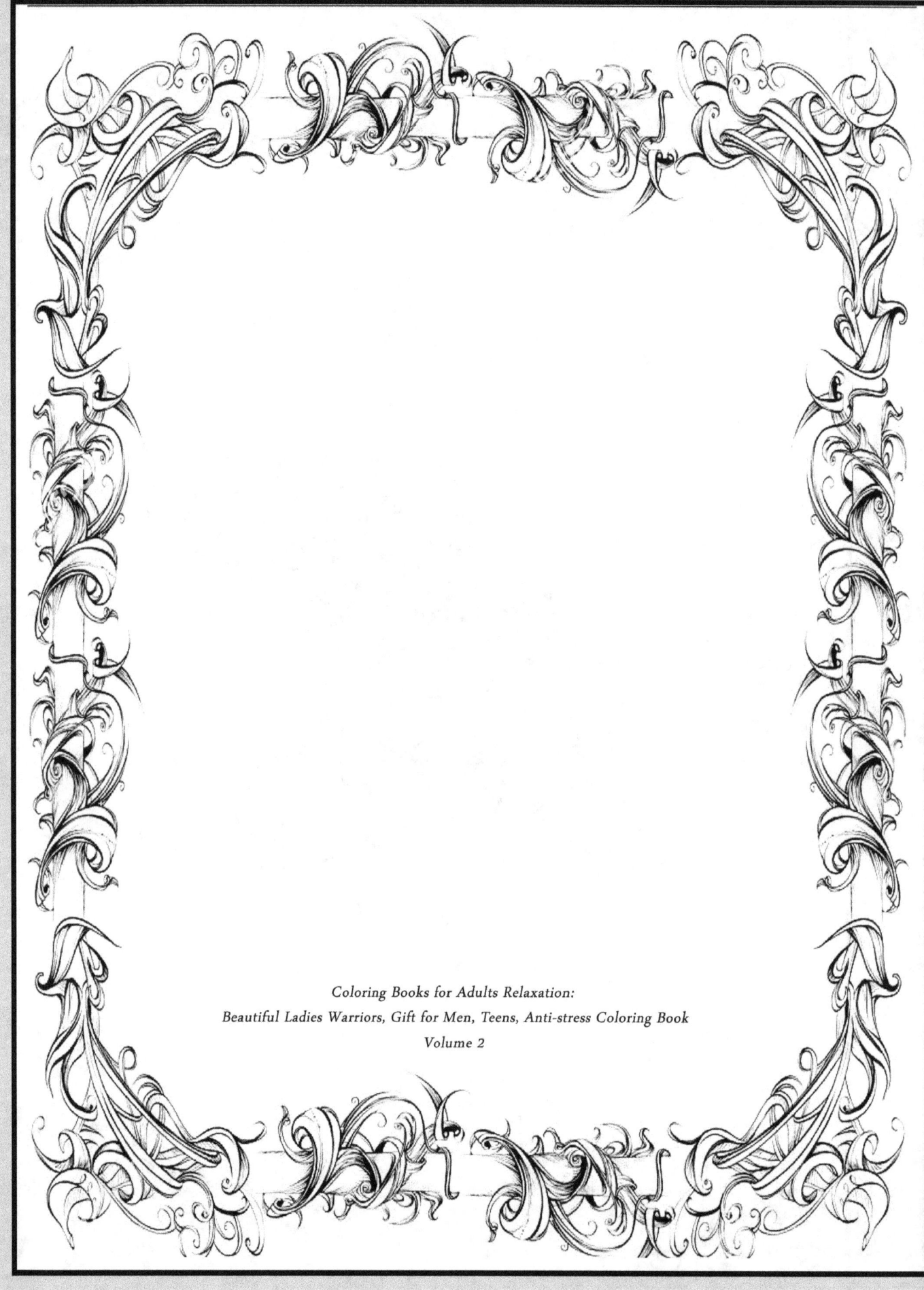

Coloring Books for Adults Relaxation:
Beautiful Ladies Warriors, Gift for Men, Teens, Anti-stress Coloring Book
Volume 2

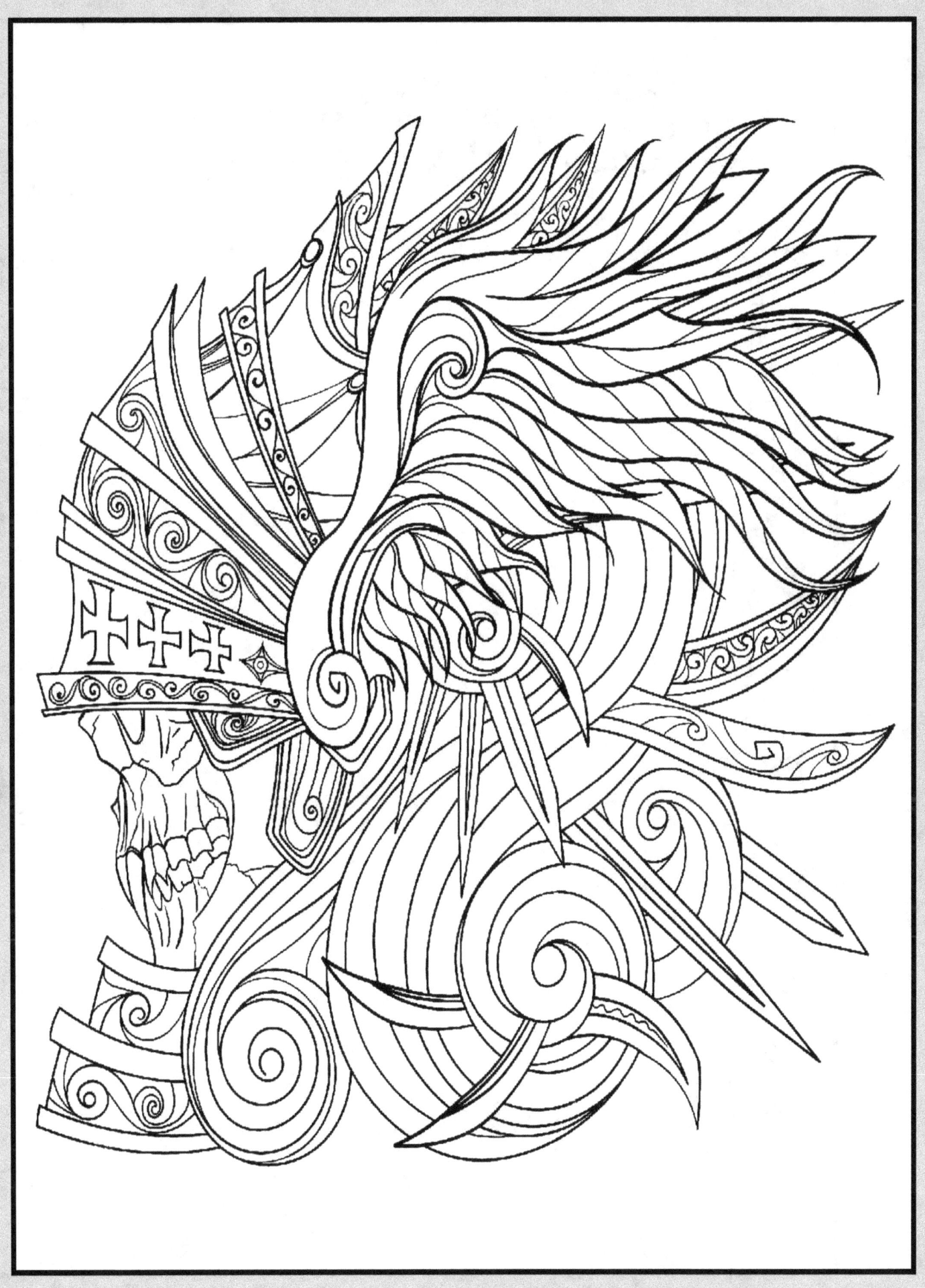

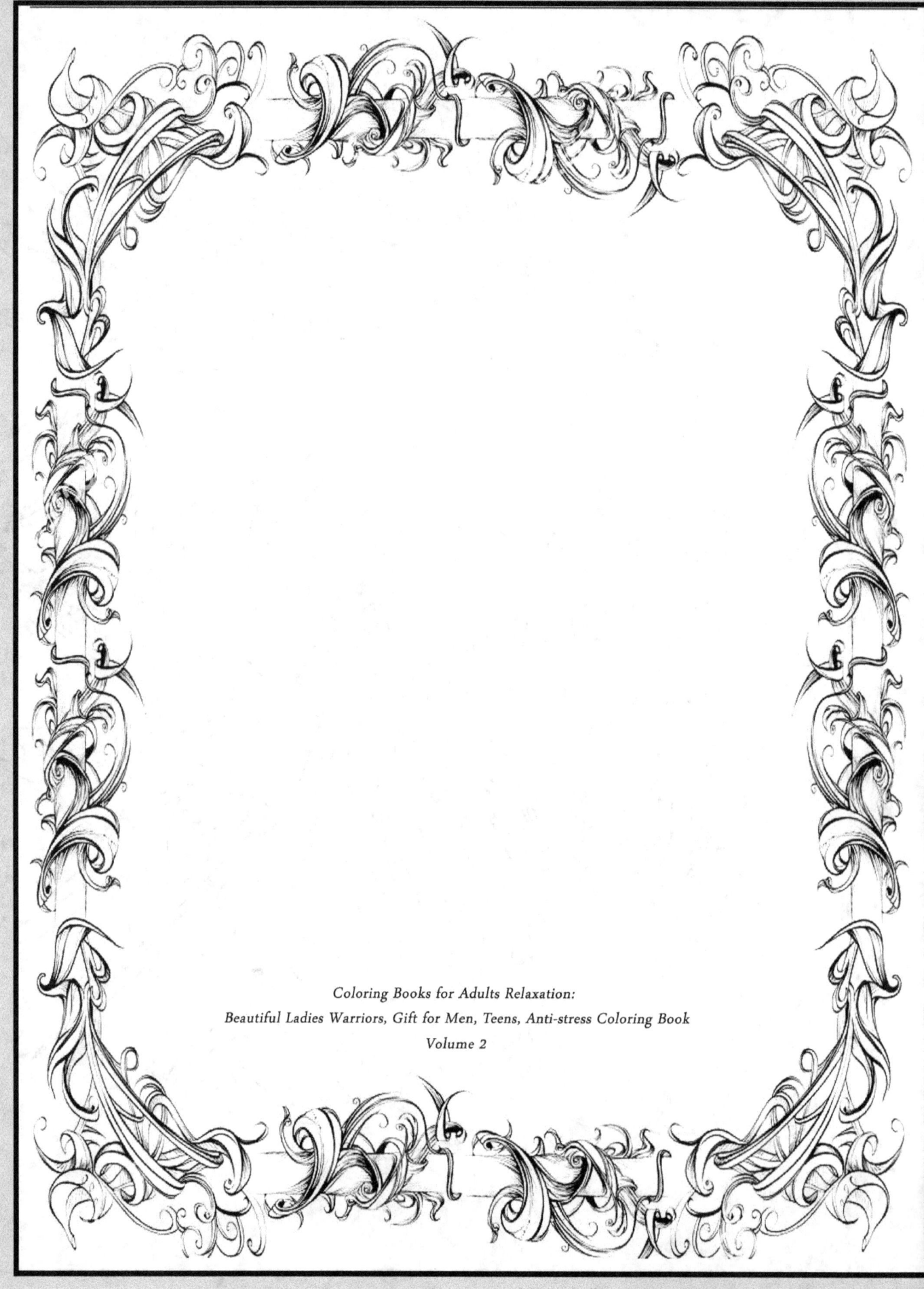

Coloring Books for Adults Relaxation:
Beautiful Ladies Warriors, Gift for Men, Teens, Anti-stress Coloring Book
Volume 2

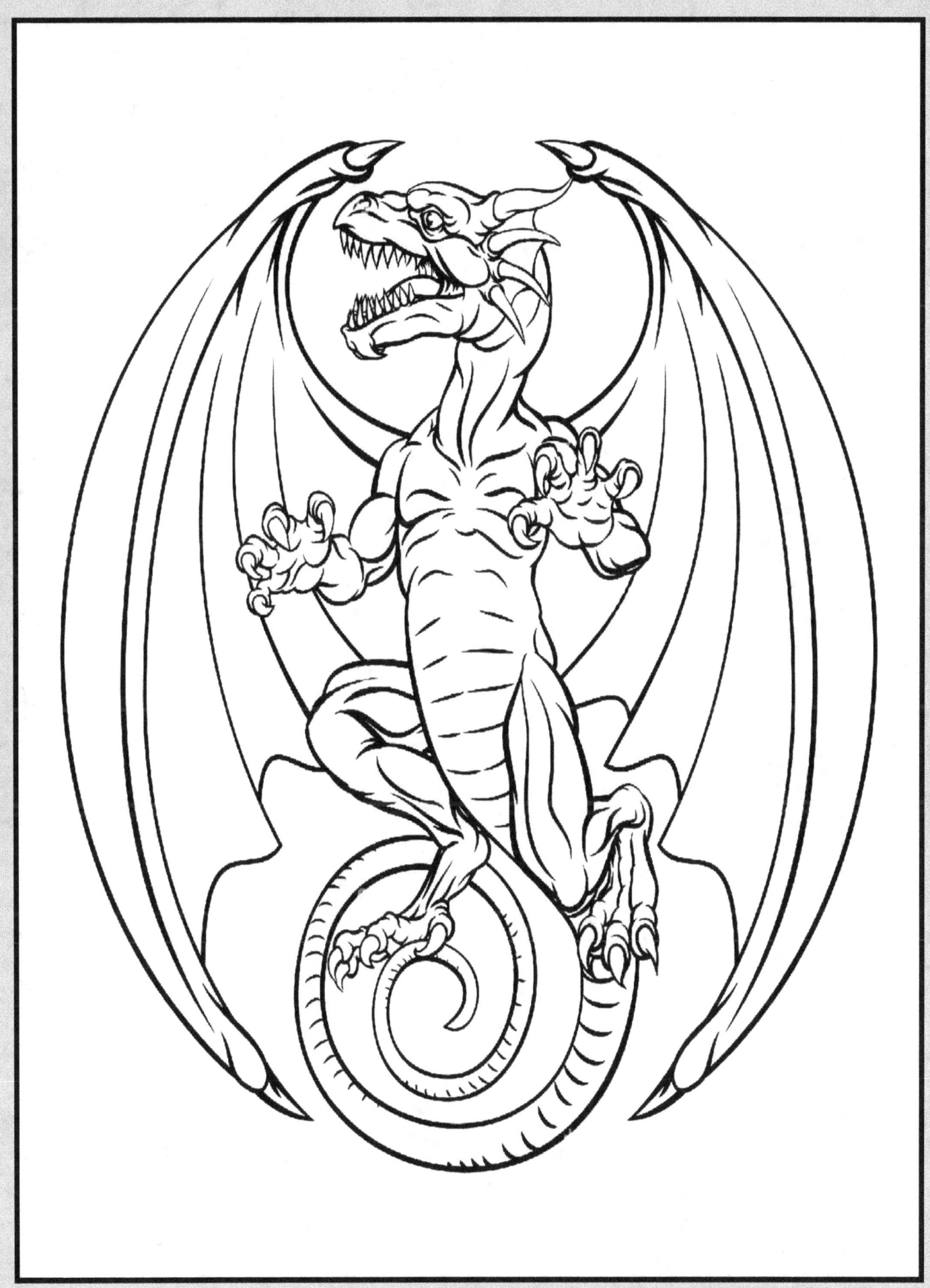

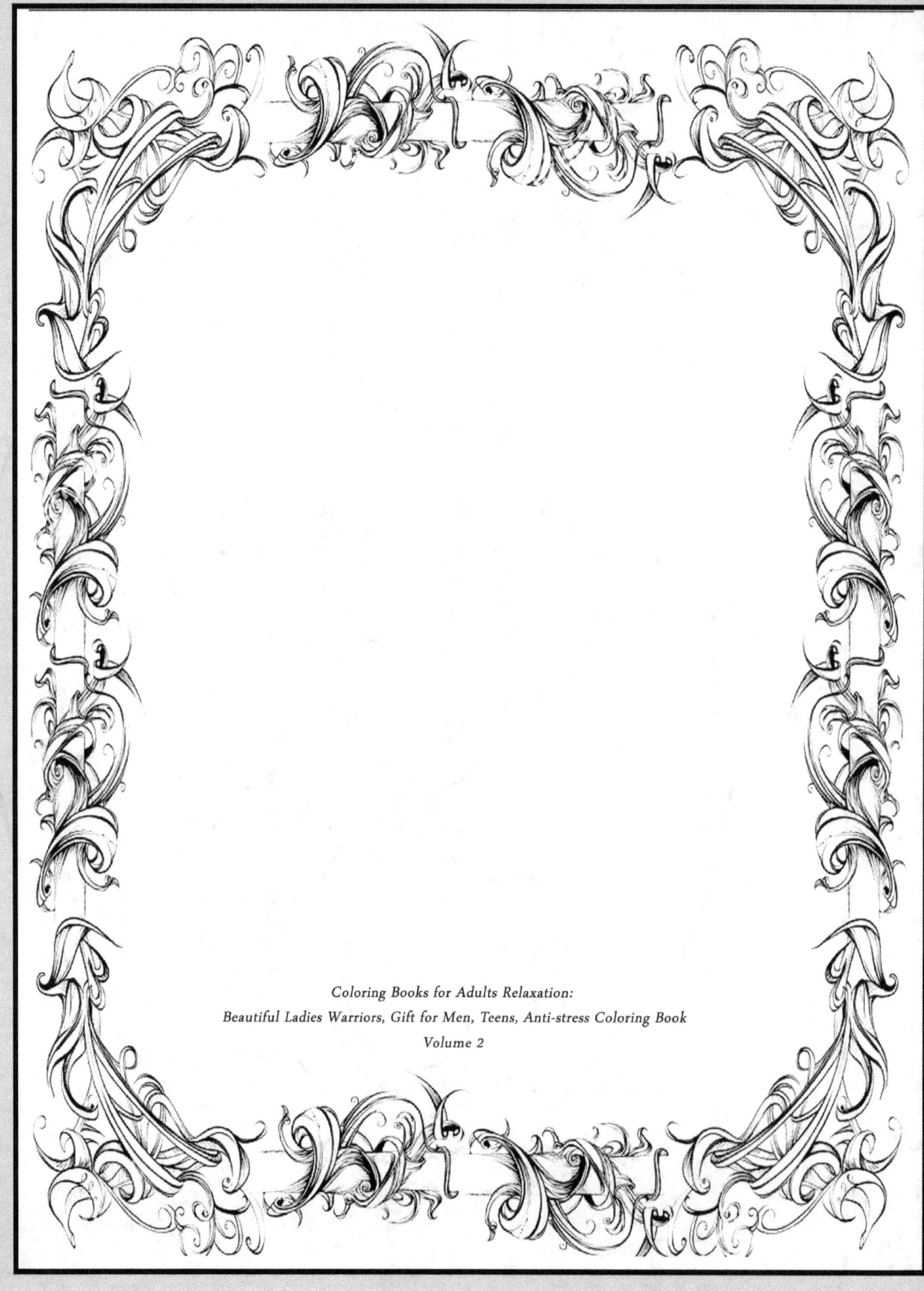

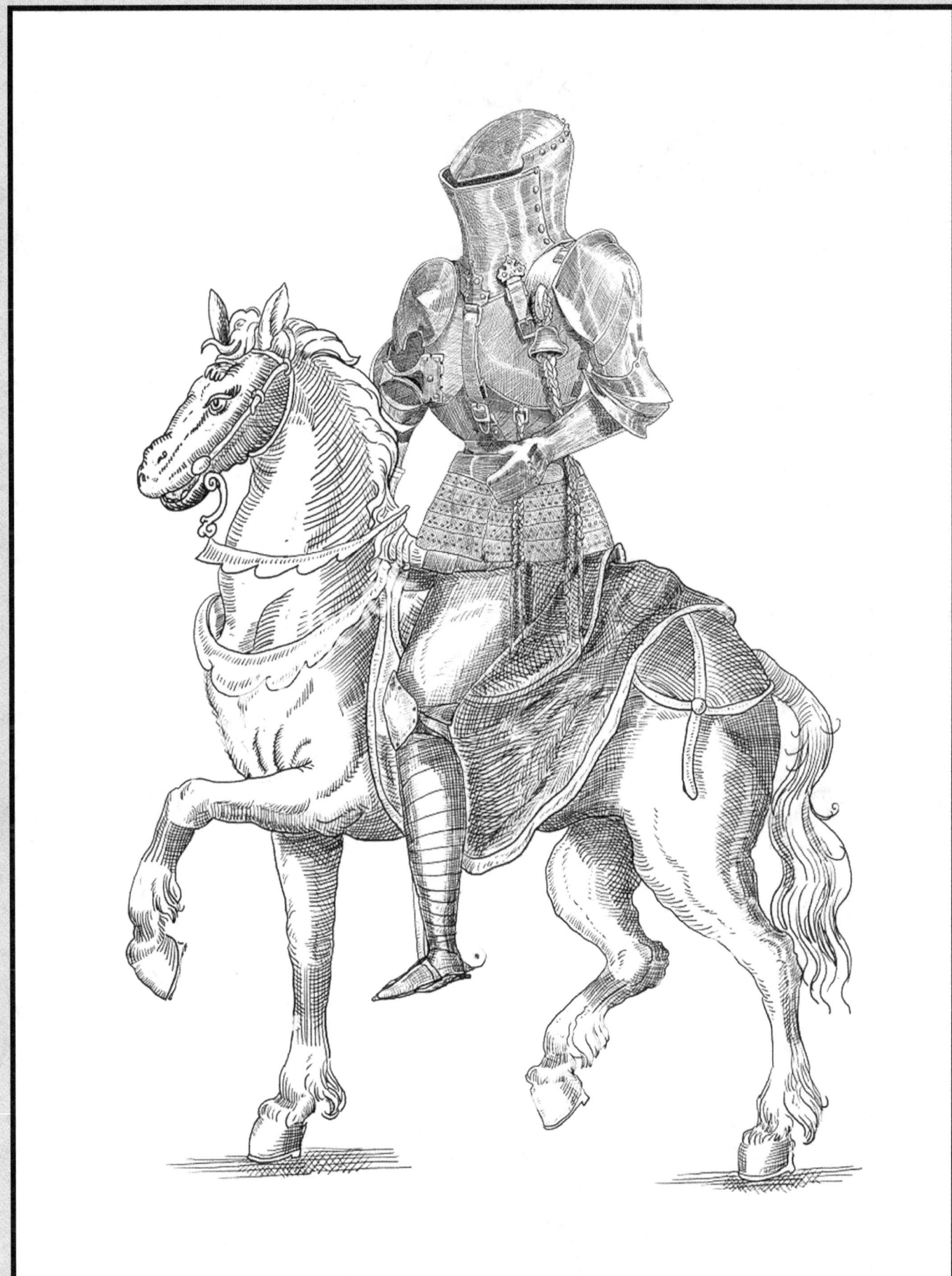

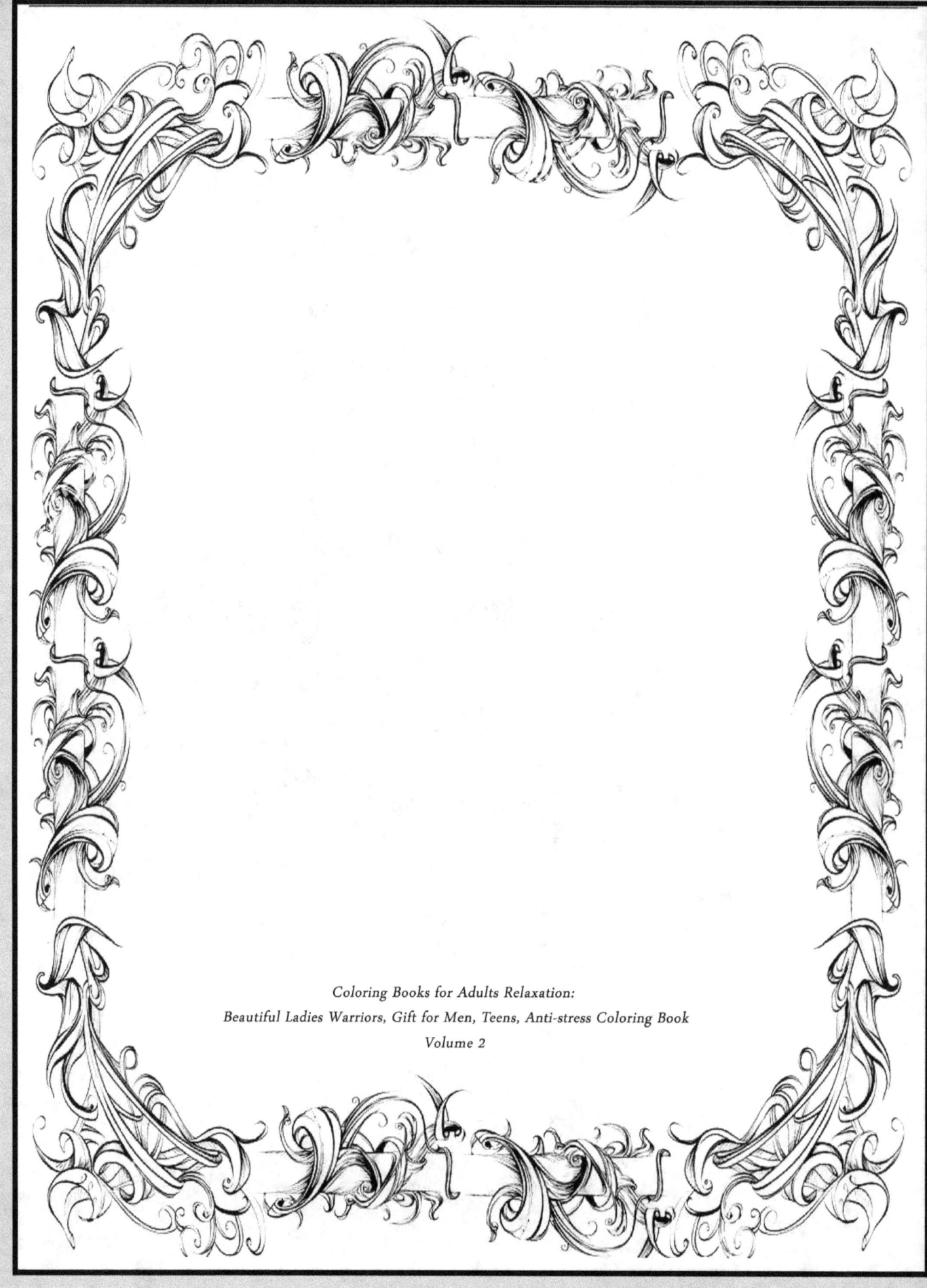

Coloring Books for Adults Relaxation:
Beautiful Ladies Warriors, Gift for Men, Teens, Anti-stress Coloring Book
Volume 2